Rivers *of* Blood
Oceans *of* Mercy

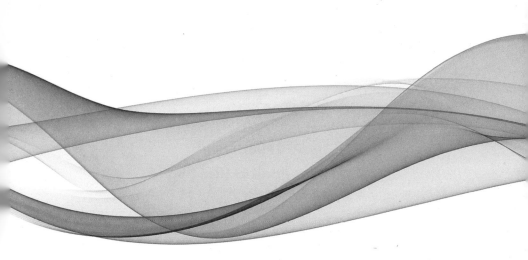

PFL PUBLISHING

Priests for Life
P.O. Box 236695
Cocoa, FL 32923
Email: Mail@PriestsForLife.org,
Phone: 321-500-1000
Visit our store: ProLifeProducts.org,
Our ministry: ProLifeCentral.org,
Support us at: ProLifeDonation.com

ISBN 978-0-578-67096-6

Rivers *of* Blood
Oceans *of* Mercy

Healing a Nation Deformed
and Divided by Abortion Loss

Kevin Burke, LSW
Theresa Burke, Ph.D
Rev. Frank Pavone

Contents

Contents *(Continued)*

Rivers *of* Blood
Oceans *of* Mercy

Kevin Burke, LSW • Theresa Burke, Ph.D • Rev. Frank Pavone

SECTION ONE:

RIVERS OF BLOOD

"The so-called right to abortion...
has sown violence and discord
at the heart of the most
intimate human relationships...
your decision [to legalize abortion]
has deformed a great nation."

– Saint Teresa of Calcutta

Kevin Burke, LSW • Theresa Burke, Ph.D • Rev. Frank Pavone

INTRODUCTION

The Traumatic Roots
of Abortion Ideology

Immediately following the 2018 confirmation hearings for Supreme Court nominee Judge Brett Kavanaugh, Democratic Strategist Alexis Grenell writes in a New York Times op-ed:

> "After a confirmation process where women all but slit their wrists, letting their stories of sexual trauma run like rivers of blood through the Capitol, the Senate still voted to confirm Judge Brett M. Kavanaugh to the Supreme Court." [1]

Grenell went on to toss a feminist grenade at those women who supported the nominee. They betrayed the cause, despite the allegations of sexual abuse directed at Kavanaugh during the hearings:

> "These women are gender traitors...the people who scare me the most are the mothers, sisters, and wives because my stupid uterus still holds out some insane hope of solidarity..."

---

1 Grenell, A. (October 6th 2018). *White Women, Come Get Your People.* NewYorkTimes.com

On Saturday, as Judge Kavanaugh was taking his oath to serve on the Supreme Court, a largely female contingent of protesters broke through a police line to the Court's chamber. They stood before the large chamber doors screaming, pounding and literally *clawing at the doors* trying to enter the chamber and disrupt the confirmation process.

The hyper-reactivity of some of the protestors reveals there is more going on here than the normal political and ideological conflicts about "reproductive rights."

We need to dig deeper.

Abortion Rights Revolutionaries - The Trauma Connection

Sexual abuse and abortion losses are two volatile experiences of trauma and complicated grief [2] that can be exploited to advance the cause of radical social movements. Without emotional and spiritual healing, some women and men with trauma in their history are vulnerable to re-direct their powerful feelings of grief, anger, and shame into radical social activism - *re-enacting* themes of their traumatic experiences.

Abortion, regardless of the circumstances, is a complex experience of loss. The powerful emotions generated from participating in the death of a child in the womb can be successfully repressed for many years for some women and men

---

2 PTSD or trauma symptoms after reproductive trauma: Seng and colleagues (2009) found that 20% of pregnant women from eight U.S. clinics had posttraumatic stress disorder (PTSD). Women were asked to identify the single worst trauma they had ever experienced, considering five types of traumatic events. The two types of trauma most frequently identified as their "worst" were past abuse and reproductive trauma. Miscarriage and abortion were specifically identified as reproductive losses that for many women were their "worst" trauma ever. –From *Recovery After Abortion*, Martha Shuping, M.D., M.A., Ashford Institute for Interdisciplinary Studies, Inc.

as they focus on educational and career pursuits. Others will turn to unhealthy behaviors, addictions, and relationships that offer a temporary escape from their buried pain.

But there are some who divert any abortion-related grief and pain, validating their own abortion decision, by *empowering* others to make the same *choice* as they did. This group played an integral role in the legalization and promotion of abortion in our nation.

In 1973 Sarah Weddington was the attorney representing the Jane Roe (Norma McCorvey) in the 1973 Roe v. Wade Supreme Court decision legalizing abortion in the United States. But years before this landmark case, in the fall of 1967, Sarah and her partner faced an unplanned pregnancy. Abortion was still illegal in Texas, so Weddington traveled to Mexico to end the life of the child in her womb.

Norma McCorvey, (the *Jane Roe* of Roe v.Wade) shared in a radio interview about her lunch meeting with Sarah Weddington in 1970.[3] Sarah was trying to convince Norma to be a plaintiff in the case. Norma already had 2 children and a failed marriage, with a family history of abuse and addiction.

Norma said in that interview that their meeting was held on the anniversary date of Sarah's abortion in Mexico.

After her personal abortion in 1967, Weddington repressed her abortion-related pain and the natural need to reconcile and heal this loss. In addition, Weddington sought to master her own traumatic loss by focusing this intense emotional energy into a movement to empower other women with the same "reproductive choice."

The lunch meeting with Norma McCorvey, the Jane Roe of

3 https://www.priestsforlife.org/audio/play.aspx?audio=lifeandchoice99-10-17

Roe v. Wade, was a powerful episode of *traumatic re-enact-ment* that contributed to the death of 60 million children in the womb as of 2019. (You will learn more about *traumatic re-enactment* in later chapters.)

Other pioneers of "reproductive rights," such as Kate Michelman, who served for many years as the director of the National Abortion Rights Action League (NARAL), and feminist Gloria Steinem, zealously promoted "reproductive rights" after their personal experience of abortion.

Leslie Blackwell of the ***Silent No More Awareness Campaign*** shares about her pro-choice activism after an abortion:

> "I discovered I was pregnant and I had just landed my dream job as a TV Talk Show Host. A roommate drove me to an abortion clinic in Greensboro, N.C. After grad-uation, I threw myself into the new job creating a façade of the perfect young career girl who had it all together ... drinking, drugging and sleeping around ... self-destruct-ing. Trying to validate my choices, I became a strong pro-abortion supporter and at times militant with anyone who didn't agree with my opinion." [4]

When Democratic Strategist Alexis Grenell writes of *rivers of blood running through the Capitol*, her "stupid uterus," and as pro-abortion radicals weaponize the intimate pain of sexual abuse to attack Judge Kavanaugh, they are unwittingly trip-ping over the truth.

The abortion procedure is often experienced by women with past sexual trauma as a type of re-enactment of that abuse. Abortion and sexual abuse are both an intimate and very painful violation of a woman's body, mind, and spirit. Both experiences leave a powerful and lasting sense of loss; loss of

---

4 https://www.silentnomoreawareness.org/testimonies/testimony.aspx?ID=3657

innocence, sense of protection, and security; with abortion the loss of a son or daughter, and the lost opportunity to parent this child.

This complicated grief can be expressed through the powerful energy of anger.

Psychologist Andy Davidson:

> "For many, being angry is more acceptable than being sad. Sad comes from hurt and we don't want to hurt anymore.
>
> We fear to expose our vulnerability, so we lash out at those around us. It could be towards someone close or a total stranger…
>
> Anger is your body's natural reaction to threat. The threat can be real or perceived. Someone died, there's nothing more threatening. While grieving, you are not yourself, you are going to misperceive a lot." [5]

Abortion rights zealots exploit the trauma of sexual abuse victims and the repressed grief and pain of women who experienced abortion loss. The political circus during the Kavanaugh hearings and the traumatic rage and pain that fed this debacle provided a very volatile and useful cover for the real agenda; protecting legalized abortion through all nine months of pregnancy.

We can see some of the same dynamics in the history of one of the key male strategists and pioneers in the movement to legalize and promote abortion in the United States.

5 Davidson, A. (July 2018). *3 Ways to Work Through the Anger Stage of Grief.* From PsychCentral. https://psychcentral.com/blog/3-ways-to-work-through-the-anger-stage-of-grief/

Kevin Burke, LSW • Theresa Burke, Ph.D • Rev. Frank Pavone

The Sins of the Father

The late Dr. Bernard Nathanson was the father of two aborted children and experienced a difficult relationship with his own father. This painful father/son relationship played a key role in the legalization and promotion of abortion in the United States.

Terry Beatley reveals in her book *"What If We've Been Wrong?"* that Nathanson's father, a highly respected obstetrician-gynecologist, was a tyrant in the home:

"Bernard was born into a loveless home in which disdain toward his mother replaced oxygen in the household. His mother was constantly and unfairly berated and belittled by her husband [His father further humiliated his wife with extramarital affairs]… Nathanson and his sister, despite this, hungered to gain their father's respect and affirmation." [6]

Nathanson's father, a staunch atheist, sent his son to the finest Jewish schools to become instructed in the letter of the law. Yet young Nathanson was immersed in a family culture where religious belief was ridiculed and faith stripped of any values and heart. As he matured Bernard was driven to find liberation from his father's oppression and emotional rejection, even as he continued to long for his father's affirmation and respect as a son, and as a man.

It is from this complex family background that Nathanson, following in his father's footsteps, entered medical school and fell in love with Ruth. Author Beatley shares that "he was drawn to her innocence, intellect, and radiance." Sadly, Nathanson would soon disfigure the beauty that attracted him to Ruth.

6 Beatley, T. (2017). *What If We've Been Wrong.* Guiding Light Books, LLC

The couple spoke of marriage but when an unplanned pregnancy occurred, Nathanson (fearing his father's response and driven to prove his self-worth) decided a newborn would interfere with the completion of his medical training. Abortion was illegal in New York at this time, so Ruth traveled alone to Montreal for the procedure.

Ruth sacrificed their child so Bernard could finish medical school. Beatley shares that she returned to New York via taxi in a puddle of blood, and as is common after an abortion, the couple soon drifted apart.

From Victim to Perpetrator

It is important to understand Nathanson's abortion in this context; the son who was *emotionally aborted* by his father, later becomes the father who aborts his unborn child. This is a complex emotional dynamic where the child who was the victim of emotional rejection and abuse, later becomes the perpetrator in the destruction of his own unborn child.

After finishing medical school and the start of his professional career, the relationship with his father became increasingly bitter and contentious. The father/son relationship was now terminated.

There is another key post-abortion dynamic to consider as Nathanson begins his professional medical career.

For Nathanson, this combination of a dysfunctional relationship with his dad, and the denial of his own post-abortion guilt and grief as a father, set the stage for his emergence as a pivotal figure in the efforts to legalize abortion in New York, and throughout the nation.

During his residency training Nathanson recognized that although abortion was illegal, by understanding how to work the system, New York City hospitals were still performing D&C abortions for supposed miscarriages – that were, in fact, healthy pregnancies. He also noted the disparity in the quality of care for patients depending on their economic background.

Nathanson's tyrannical father led him to share a natural affinity for the anti-establishment, anti-authority culture of the 1960s. He despised the medical establishment's maintenance of what he saw as an unjust and unsafe tolerance of illegal abortion.

As an ob-gyn physician, Nathanson became an essential frontman in the campaign to repeal existing abortion laws. Author Terry Beatley details in her book the unfolding events and key players (and the use of deception, misinformation and outright lies) leading up to the legalization of abortion; first in New York in 1970 and then with the Roe v. Wade Supreme Court decision in 1973 legalizing abortion in all 50 states.

The Apple in the Garden of Choice

Whatever Nathanson's good intentions, once you begin the descent down that slippery slope where medical professionals and parents assume the life and death decisions that are the exclusive providence of the Creator of life, a process of moral and spiritual corruption and decay sets in.

After abortion became legal in New York in 1970, Dr. Nathanson trained doctors in the use of vacuum abortion, a method recently perfected at that time in communist China, as a more efficient method of termination. He also shared with his fellow physician's abortion methods for later-term pregnancies such as saline abortion.

This method injects a poisonous saline solution into the mother's womb. The child inhales the solution into their tiny lungs as the saline burns the baby's skin. The child suffers gruesome and painful torture for about an hour before dying in the womb. The mother gives birth to a dead child, or in some cases to a child barely alive which is abandoned or in some cases left to die.

As disturbing as this is, there is an even more shocking event in the journey of Bernard Nathanson as a pioneer of abortion rights. Dr. Nathanson, who as a young medical student persuaded Ruth to abort their child, and was emotionally aborted by his father, assumed a dark mastery of his repressed grief and pain.

Nathanson devolves into a sinister reflection of his tyrannical father

Author Terry Beatley shares that Dr. Nathanson was involved in another unplanned pregnancy after Ruth. This time, the doctor personally performed the abortion of his unborn child:

> "Yes, his hands had personally killed his own child and, when he had finished the procedure, he felt only pride in his adept skill."

The Crushing Burden of Truth

The development of ultrasound technology finally broke through Nathanson's denial of the humanity of the unborn child. He came to reject abortion and regret his role in the legalization of the procedure, and his personal responsibility, directly or indirectly, for some 75,000 abortions.

Fr. Frank Pavone knew Dr. Nathanson and introduced him at an international pro-life presentation in 1994 at which Dr. Nathanson announced that he was becoming a Christian. He said at the end, "I hope God can forgive me," and Fr. Frank assured him that God, seeing his repentance, had already done so, and the whole assembly prayed for him right then and there.

Nearly two decades later, in 2011, Fr. Frank visited Dr. Nathanson in his Manhattan apartment just days before his death. His voice just at a whisper, the first thing he said to Fr. Frank when he entered his room was, "Fr. Frank, how goes the crusade?" There, in the final days of Dr. Nathanson's final illness, his mind was focused on the pro-life activists working to undo the damage he had done. He wanted to encourage all who work to heal the wounds which he knew he had done so much to unleash.

Healing Our National Trauma - The Road to Recovery

Rivers of Blood/Oceans of Mercy will help you get beyond the contentious political, moral and theological debates, and get to the heart of the issue. This will equip you as a minister, counselor, friend, and family member to reach out with the understanding and mercy of the Lord to those hurting after abortion, and speak the truth in love to a nation in massive denial of what is, given the widespread impact of abortion, a *national trauma*. You will be empowered to speak, teach and preach on this topic without fear, and with great sensitivity and effectiveness.

We will explore the connection of abortion with previous trauma such as divorce and abuse, the rising transgender madness, and how the high rates of abortion impact our poorest communities. Despite the institutionalized censorship, you will read how some very popular television and film allow the powerful expression of themes closely associated with this national trauma.

When we get beyond the rhetoric of *reproductive rights*, you will discover that the experience of abortion touches on the most intimate aspects of personal identity, wounding the hearts and souls of women and men.

You will also find as our journey unfolds, the good news of God's mercy and restoration. Women and men that experience this mercy, reconciliation, and healing of God our Creator, do indeed become, as St John Paul II proclaimed, "... *among the most eloquent defenders of everyone's right to life."*[7]

---

7 *Evangelium Vitae* (The Gospel of Life), #99

Kevin Burke, LSW • Theresa Burke, Ph.D • Rev. Frank Pavone

CHAPTER ONE

Abortion Stigma and the "Great Divide"

Abortion activists like the late Dr. Bernard Nathanson have removed the barriers to abortion. Yet, 47 years after the legalization of abortion, and over 60 million procedures as of 2020, researchers and public health officials note the persistence of stigma associated with abortion:

> "... abortion stigma can be observed at the individual level by measuring worries about the judgment by others, isolation, self-judgment (such as shame), and perceptions of community condemnation. (Cockrill et al., 2013)" [8]

Leila Hessini, writing in *Rewire*, takes it one step further and says that abortion stigma is a form of discrimination:

> "Abortion stigma occurs when people are labeled, dehumanized, or discriminated against due to their need for, or association with, abortion." [9]

Students at Loyola University participated in a Student's

---

8 Cockrill, K. *Commentary: Imagine a World Without Abortion Stigma.* Women & Health, 54:7 (2014) 662-665.

9 Hessini, L. (September 28, 2016). *Destigmatizing and Decriminalizing Abortion: That's Our Collective.* Rewire.News.com

for Reproductive Choice activity with a papaya to help *de-stigmatize* abortion:

> "Students used a papaya to learn about vacuum aspiration abortions, claiming it's similar to sucking out papaya seeds …The purpose of the papaya workshop is for students to learn about aspiration abortions, and to destigmatize abortion in general." [10]

Kate Cockrill, MPH is the co-founder of *Sea Change*, whose mission is to "transform the culture of reproductive stigma." The Sea Change website asks some questions about abortion stigma:

> – Why is abortion so hard to talk about?

> – Why does getting an abortion often feel illicit and shameful?

> – Why don't we hear about the abortion experiences of our mothers, sisters, friends?

Cockrill and her colleagues talk about strategies to reduce and eliminate abortion stigma with the goal of lessening a woman's isolation and building connection, social support, and validation of their abortion decision:

> "We can imagine a world in which abortion stigma and shame do not taint the relationships of people with abortion experiences … People might talk regularly about their abortion experiences with co-workers, friends, and family members…"

Reduce the secrecy, remove the shame, guilt and silence, and women are supported and empowered by their reproductive

10 Michelle-Hanson, S. (October 11, 2016). *Group at Catholic University Tries to Destigmatize Abortion by Practicing on Fruit.* LiveActionNews.org

choices. Abortion is just another in a series of life events and transitions that women can safely negotiate and share with friends and family.

Yet even here in the United States, where abortion is displayed in media and television in a positive light[11], most of the women and men who experience this medical procedure keep it a closely guarded secret.

So what's going on here?

As abortion rights researcher Kate Cockrill asks, why is abortion so hard to talk about and feel illicit and shameful? Are the problems abortion stigma and discrimination against those that have the procedure?

Closer to the Heart

Abortion has been a divisive issue in our society since the Roe v. Wade decision of 1973 that legalized the procedure. We tend to think of this *great divide* as originating in the stark differences in religion, politics, and morality concerning abortion. These are clearly the public manifestation of the fault lines that quickly surfaced across our national landscape after Roe v. Wade.

But there is a deeper *disconnection and fragmentation* in the lives of those women and men that participate in abortion decisions and procedures. As we examine the emotional and spiritual fallout from abortion, you will learn how the heart of recovery is providing a way to restore integration and

11 *Abortion Bias Seeps Into News.* Groups.csail.mit.edu [A four-part study in the Los Angeles Times, Sunday, July 1-4, 1990 of major newspaper, television and newsmagazine coverage over 18 months, including more than 100 interviews with journalists and with activists on both sides of the abortion debate, confirms that this bias often exists.]

Kevin Burke, LSW • Theresa Burke, Ph.D • Rev. Frank Pavone

connection - wholeness and holiness.

Our journey to understand and heal abortion loss begins with a great paradox in the foundation of pro-abortion philosophy and rhetoric. Those who promote *"reproductive rights"* have been very successful in presenting the issue as a sacrosanct, very private and personal issue; we must be very careful not to interfere as a woman makes her reproductive decisions. Because after all... *it's her body, her choice.*

Yet, the female body is anything but "pro-choice."

When a woman becomes pregnant, and the baby is developing normally, everything in her body is gearing up to welcome the new life within her. At conception, a complex and very natural transformation begins designed to protect and nurture this developing life, regardless of the circumstances. The pro-abortion language of rights and physical autonomy is clearly at odds with the natural response of the female body to a healthy pregnancy.

We know all pregnancies are not planned or welcome. While the body may be clear of its task, the mind and heart can be filled with confusion and anxiety. Here are some common reactions from women and men facing an unplanned pregnancy and discerning abortion:

> – Is this really a good time for me to bring a child into the world? I don't feel prepared to be a mom/dad right now.

> – This guy is already squirming and I am going to be stuck with this baby. I need to abort.

> – I want to finish college first and get established in my career.

18

– I was date raped and traumatized…I can't have this baby.

– My family and friends, including the father of the baby, tell me abortion is the best thing for everyone. I don't know what to do and feel pressured to make a decision. I don't feel like I really have a choice.

Emotional Abortion

Pregnant parents can be desperate to turn-back time and restore life to a pre-pregnancy state, and abortion seems to promise that simple solution.

The truth is abortion, like giving birth, is a life-changing event for those that are closely connected to the child's death.

In the decision-making process after the discovery of pregnancy up until the abortion procedure itself, we find the epicenter of the abortion shockwave. This is true for those who seem to approach the decision with relative ease and appear on the surface to have no immediate post-abortion reactions.

It is equally and powerfully apparent with abortion decisions that are fraught with ambivalence, anxiety and in some cases different levels of manipulation and coercion from others. There is a wide continuum of pre and post-abortion reactions reflecting the diverse personality and history of each person.

Regardless of these differences, an important emotional disconnection takes place once the possibility of abortion enters the conscious mind; this is the beginning of an *emotional abortion* within the parental heart - or within the heart of a grandparent, sibling, aunt, or another family member who is part of an abortion decision:

– This denial, whether conscious or unconscious, is the beginning of a disconnection between the natural relationship bond of a parent for their developing child and a very powerful need to deny or repress this truth of the human heart.

– Emotional survival after abortion requires a disconnection from your body, heart, and soul; a denial and repression of the emotional and biological truth of what has been lost.

– The denial of the deeper emotional pain and loss of abortion make it challenging to grieve and integrate this experience into one's life.

– This relational disconnection is the source of many of the symptoms suffered after abortion for both women and men as they cope with the painful and conflictual feelings and memories of the abortion event.

Abortion is not a normal experience of loss. It is *complicated grief.*

"…every time I look at my children I have now, I think about that little face I never saw and the child I have never known." – Aimee

With a normal experience of loss, you are provided the opportunity to acknowledge that there has been a death and find support moving through that experience. There are religious rituals, family and social supports, expressions of concern and compassion that all help in the grieving process.

After an abortion, emotions often remain shrouded in shame and secrecy. At times this grief and pain seek an outlet. This may be manifest in symptoms such as anxiety/depression and immune system disorders.[12] Sometimes the need to suppress and cope with this pain can lead to different forms of self-medication with drugs, food, promiscuity, and other impulsive behavior. [13] We can even see addictions as a symptom of this "relational wound" as people enter into unhealthy attachments/relationships with substances, food, abusive/exploitive partners, work, and pornography.

Many women and men appear to rebound quickly after the abortion event as they return to school and work commitments. They dive enthusiastically into our increasingly hyper-busy, technology-saturated world that is perfectly designed for distraction and dissociation. But over time this can come at a great personal cost with complications that can impact health, and marriage and family life.

An abortion healing program helps restore the broken relationship with the aborted child or children, and reduce the power of unhealthy, addictive relationships and other self-destructive behaviors. As you will learn in our upcoming chapters on healing, the reclamation of this *aborted love* and the restoration of a strong emotional and spiritual relationship with the aborted child (or children,) is the foundation of the recovery process.

---

12 Rue, V and Coyle, C. *The Alliance for Post Abortion Research and Training.* StandApart.org

13 Theresa Burke and David C. Reardon. *Forbidden Grief: The Unspoken Pain of Abortion.* Springfield, IL: Acorn Books, 2007.

Kevin Burke, LSW • Theresa Burke, Ph.D • Rev. Frank Pavone

CHAPTER TWO

A Traumatic Experience of Loss

The author Karen Blixen once said, "All sorrows can be borne if you put them into a story or tell a story about them." But what if a person can't tell a story about his sorrows? What if his story tells him? – Stephen Grosz

Emotional trauma results from a deeply painful experience that overwhelms a person's normal coping skills. Key features of traumatic loss include the following:

– The traumatic event involves exposure to a situation where death or serious injury occurs, accompanied by feelings of fear, helplessness, and horror at the time of the trauma:

"It was on February 25th, 1995 that my life changed forever. Andrea had gone to the clinic and had an abortion while I was at work. Her sister paid for the procedure and was the one who told me that it was done. The last thing I remember after hearing the news was lying in the parking lot of a bar screaming at the top of my lungs. I have no recollection of how I got home or how many days passed before I moved back in with my parents." – Jason

– Individuals experience flashbacks and nightmares of their procedure and the avoidance of sights, sounds, smells or feelings associated with the trauma.

> "I had nightmares after the abortion. I avoided driving near the abortion center. When I ran the vacuum in my apartment soon after the procedure I was hit with a wave of panic and anxiety - it reminded me of the suction machine. My sister just had a baby shower and I had to hide my grief and pain and try to share in her excitement and joy." – Susan

– During periods of heightened anxiety and depression, suicidal thoughts can occur. The wounded soul will try to numb those painful feelings and memories through substance abuse and other addictive and/or impulsive behavior, such as binge shopping and promiscuity.

Other self-destructive behaviors serve as an outlet for buried rage, grief and hurt and/or self-punishment about the abortion loss. This can include forms of self-injury, poor relationship choices, and relationship instability featuring cycles of rage and rejection.

> "I had my abortion freshman year of college. My boyfriend was clear that abortion was the only option, and I reluctantly agreed. Soon after we broke up and I became the party girl and starting drinking a lot and sleeping around…something I never did prior to the abortion. Sadly this led to another unplanned pregnancy and abortion before I got a hold of my drinking and became less promiscuous. I went on to get my nursing degree, marry and have a family. But the darkness and pain from that time were still there, buried deep inside of me." – Joanne

Traumatic Repetition

An especially troubling and misunderstood complication of abortion is the phenomena of traumatic repetition.

"Data from the 39 areas that reported the number of previous abortions for women who obtained abortions in 2015 indicate that the majority (56.3%) had no previous abortions, 35.4% had one or two previous abortions, and 8.2% had three or more previous abortions."[14]

The *Population Research Institute* reports that the average Russian woman has seven abortions in her lifetime.[15] Common reactions to women who have multiple procedures:

– Are these women using abortion as a type of birth control?

– Why haven't they learned from their first time on the abortion table to not get themselves in this mess again?

In the following excerpt from the book ***Forbidden Grief,*** therapist Theresa Burke sheds some light on the problem of repeat abortions:

"Christine had her first abortion at the age of 18. She was under treatment for mild depression, and her psychiatrist recommended abortion. Since this was before 1973 and *Roe V Wade*, Christine was told that she would have to sign a paper that stated she would commit suicide if she did not have an abortion. Her mental health care workers orchestrated the entire event. In reality, Christine knew she would not kill herself, but she felt that she had to follow her doctor's orders.

14 The Center for Disease Control. https://www.cdc.gov/mmwr/volumes/67/ss/ss6713a1.htm

15 Mosher, S. and Elizabeth, C. (2012). *Will Russia Come Back to Life?* Population Research Institute. Pop.org

She later married and became pregnant again at the age of 22. Her husband was eager and ready to be a family, but she felt anxiety and fear over becoming a parent. The message from her psychiatrist that colored her view of herself as a potential mother was that she was not mentally stable enough to have a child and that having a baby would provoke a mental breakdown and even suicidal behavior. The thought of having a baby simply terrified her. Because of her fears of inadequacy, she had another abortion and divorced shortly thereafter.

Christine's third pregnancy also ended in second-trimester abortion. This pattern continued three more times for a total of six abortions. Each time she had an intense desire to be a mother, but each time she could see no other recourse but abortion, reenacting the first trauma of helplessness to overcome her perceived inadequacy and incompetence…Christine is not alone… This problem of repeat abortions is not due to callousness or the careless use of birth control. Instead, it is far more likely that women who have multiple abortions are caught in a pattern of reenacting their traumatic abortions. A central aspect of trauma is a sense of helplessness. Reenactment is a means by which individuals revisit their traumas, repeatedly returning to the same traumatic situation…"

You can read in much greater detail, with instructive case studies about abortion trauma in *Forbidden Grief: The Unspoken Pain of Abortion.*[16]

The Abortion Pill

---

16 Burke, T. and Reardon, D. (2007). *Forbidden Grief: The Unspoken Pain of Abortion.* Springfield, IL: Acorn Books.

In March 2016 the FDA approved the use of the abortion pill, Mifepristone for women up to 10 weeks pregnant. Close to 40% percent of abortions in the United States are chemical abortions and this number will likely continue to rise.

Couples often rationalize that the abortion pill merely initiates an early miscarriage. They are tempted to see the pills as an easier solution than a medical procedure at the abortion center. However, the actual experience of the abortion pill can be a shocking and traumatic event.

A woman shares her experience:

"I was 6 weeks pregnant and after an extended period of severe cramping, the child was delivered in our bathroom. My partner had to fish the tiny child out of the toilet."

The father buried the child in their back yard. He frequently visited the "gravesite" as he struggled to process the grief and trauma of that event. They found significant emotional and spiritual healing of that experience by attending an abortion healing program, but they remain wounded by that abortion individually, and as a couple.

What are the possible psychological and physical trauma associated with chemical abortion in the home?

Counselor Cullen Herout shares:

> "...if we acknowledge that some women experience traumatic responses to abortion, it is equally vital to acknowledge that with a medical abortion, the locus of that trauma moves from a surgical center to the woman's home... Sensory stimuli associated with the traumatic experience might trigger acute anxiety, disturbing mental images or other negative sensory flashbacks. Sometimes

these triggers happen consciously, and sometimes they do not. But if a woman has a negative abortion experience, she is likely to develop negative thoughts and emotions that can be triggered by any reminders of that experience.

If the locus of a negative abortion experience is a surgical center, it is less difficult to avoid triggers that might elicit negative thoughts or emotions. If driving by the abortion clinic on the way home from work brings anxiety, it is easy to take a different route home. If reminders of the sound of the abortion machine bring a sense of panic, it is easy to escape a situation and move oneself to a different location.

We need to increase our efforts to educate the public about the reality of chemical abortion. Women and their partners need to understand the psychological risks of at-home abortions and the likely individual and relational impact of labor and delivery of early pregnancies in the home. – *Crisis Magazine* [17]

---

17 Herout, C. (April 7, 2017). *Trauma Associated with Do-it-yourself Abortions* Crisis Magazine. Crisismagazine.com

CHAPTER THREE

Stranger Things and Stephen King

For now we see through a glass, darkly;
– 1Corinthians 13:12

"The artist...one who allows art to realize its purposes through him...a vehicle and molder of the unconscious psychic life of mankind."
– Psychiatrist Carl Jung, Psychology and Literature, 1930.

In the popular Netflix series *Stranger Things* we learn of a secret government program during the 1980s in Hawkins Indiana. Here in this government laboratory, scientists perform human experiments to develop special mental powers, such as the ability to move objects with the mind and travel to different dimensions. While some volunteered for the project others were kidnapped and held as prisoners.

Two of the subjects included a pregnant mother named Terry and her daughter. This child, known as Eleven (from the number tattooed on her wrist) was taken during birth and separated from her mother. Terry was told the baby died in childbirth. The mother suspected otherwise and as she came closer to the truth she was given strong doses of shock treatment to silence her.

Using familiar themes found in science fiction and the Bible's book of Genesis, *Stranger Things* tells a tale of how mankind's pride opens the door to evil. As Eleven (aka El) grew into early adolescence at the government laboratory, she cultivated strong mental powers. Through special experiments, she developed the ability to travel to other dimensions and move large objects with her mind.

In one experiment, El travels into an altered reality. She is transported to the other side of the world where she encounters a Russian spy and gathers intelligence information for the government. But this experiment opened the door to a shadowy reflection of their small Midwestern town of Hawkins Indiana called the *Upside Down World*. A monster from the Upside Down World enters the town of Hawkins through portals created by the experiment.

The creature is a living and very intelligent virus. The monster has large tentacles and spider webs of flesh and goo that trap its prey. The creature then enters through the mouth and slowly sucks out the life of its victim. One of the early targets of the virus is Will, played by Noah Schnapp. Will is part of a group of middle school boys who share a strong bond of friendship, and a special love for the fantasy game *Dungeon and Dragons*.

The monster snatches Will from his garden shed and takes him to the upside-down world. When Will goes missing after his encounter with the monster, he is presumed dead by the police and citizens of Hawkins.

Will's single mother Joyce, played by Wynona Rider, is convinced her missing son is alive. Will is able to communicate with his mother while trapped in the Upside Down World by using his mind. He sends messages to his mom at their home by making lights pulsate and through manipulating household appliances like the phone and boom box.

In one very moving scene, Joyce is nestled inside a cabinet in her living room. She cradles a bundle of flashing Christmas lights close to her heart. The lights convince her that Will is alive. She is desperate to rescue him from danger and won't let anything stop her.

Joyce declares:

> *"I don't care if anyone believes me; I won't stop until I find my boy."*

Others in the small Hawkins Indiana community think she has lost her mind with grief and is unable to accept the death of her son.

The Abortion Monster

A series like Stranger Things can serve as a vehicle to express what is kept hidden in a community and culture. Stories can help give a voice to buried grief and painful emotions. They can touch those dark shadowy places in our own *Upside Down Worlds.*

The episodes have a number of references to the politics, music, and culture of the 1980s. But the themes of missing and endangered children found in *Stranger Things* plugs into another disturbing fact about that decade.

In the 1980s the national abortion rate was rising.[18] In towns and cities across the U.S. - *millions of children were missing:*

18 O'Bannon, R. (2003). *Abortion Statistics and Trends over the Past Thirty Years.* NRLC.org

– Abortion crossed the 1.5 million a year mark for the
first time in 1980 with 1,553,900 procedures.

– The U.S. abortion ratio reached its peak in 1984, with
364 abortions for every thousand live births.

– The high mark since the legalization of abortion in
1973 occurred in 1988 with 1,590,800 procedures.

Every day in abortion centers across our nation, abortionists
do a procedure that is very similar to the methods used by
the monster of *Stranger Things*. The doctor uses a vacuum
abortion machine that enters the womb of a woman and
sucks out a living unborn baby. In later-term procedures,
the abortionist dismembers the living child in the womb and
removes the body parts of a fully formed boy or girl.

And then there is the impact on the mothers and fathers who
participate in the death of their unborn children. Listen to
a woman who had an abortion freshman year of college and
her experience of watching *Stranger Things*:

"When I watched the separation of El from her mother
at birth, it connected me to so many painful memories
and anger about my abortion that were buried deep in
my past. It brought back to how the abortion procedure
separated me from my baby."

A woman who felt pressured by her parents and boyfriend to
abort her child shares:

"I was really drawn to Joyce. She knew her son was alive.
In that scene where she is holding the Christmas lights
and trying to connect with her son…I found myself
weeping once again for my child I lost to abortion. For
many years after the abortion, I was drinking too much
and in bad relationships. I was missing my child. I

needed to connect with my baby and know he was ok.
I did find that peace when I went through a healing
program for abortion loss."

"Are We Just Going to Pretend It Didn't Happen?"

Another popular book and movie set in the 1980s touch
on some powerful abortion-related themes. A new screen
adaptation of Stephen King's classic 1986 novel "It" came
to theaters in 2017. It was a record-setting debut for a
September film grossing an estimated $123.1 million.

King's story explores the small New England town of Deery
and a group of geeky adolescents called *The Losers*. As the
story unfolds they encounter vicious bullies and disappearing
classmates.

Something dark and mysterious is happening in the town of
Deery:

– The murder rate in Deery is six times that of any other
town of comparable size in New England

– Children disappear at a rate of forty to sixty per year
and their bodies are never found.

One member of the Losers, Mike Hanlon, says the town is in
a state of mass denial about this disturbing phenomenon:

"In Deery, people have a way of looking the other way."

In the opening sequence of the movie, a young boy named
Georgie is attempting to retrieve his toy boat which floated
down a storm drain.

King's book describes Georgie's encounter with the clown
named Pennywise, lurking beneath the surface of the storm

drain:

> "Want your boat, Georgie?' Pennywise asked…he held it up, smiling.

> 'Yes, sure,' George said, looking into the storm drain… Georgie reached. The clown seized his arm. And George saw the clown's face change…"

Dave hears the desperate screams of Georgie:

> Dave Gardener was the first to get there… Blood flowed into the storm drain from the tattered hole where [Georgie's] left arm had been. A knob of bone, horribly bright, peeked through the torn cloth."

A mangled arm is all that is left of little Georgie.

Months later after Georgie's disappearance, his brother Bill is driven to find the boy's missing body. Bill leads his friends Ritchie, Eddie, and Stan into trouble as they search the sewers for some sign of the boy.

The children learn that a demonic clown with razor-like teeth they name "It" lives in the sewers beneath the town. The clown periodically surfaces to visit children in different monstrous forms tailored to their personal fears.

Missing Fathers and Missing Children

Stephen's King biography reveals childhood trauma and father loss that left the young boy tortured by anxiety and phobias. Writing became a creative outlet for his emotional pain that King skillfully wove into his tales of horror, science fiction, and fantasy. [19]

19 Leafe, D. (May12, 2009). *Stephen King's Real Horror Story: How the novelist's addiction to drink and drugs nearly killed him* by David Leafe. The Daily Mail UK. DailyMail.co.uk

As Psychiatrist Carl Jung suggests, a gifted storyteller like King, who experienced a daily and intensive compulsion to write, can connect to those dark currents submerged in a community and culture.

Like the clown Pennywise lurking beneath the sewers, there are sinister forces and events that the adults and society fail to recognize, or aggressively deny. As Mike Hanlon said of the town of Deery, "people have a way of looking the other way."

One of the Losers Bill asks his friends after Georgie's attack:

> "What happens when another Georgie goes missing? Are we just going to pretend it didn't happen, like everyone else in this town?"

We often fail to acknowledge that children born since abortion was legalized in 1973 are "abortion survivors." Some have expressed an intuitive sense that children in their families and communities were missing.

Psychiatrist Dr. Philip Ney has studied and treated children and adults who learned at some point in their lives that their sibling or half-sibling was aborted.

Author Janet Morana shares:

> "....Dr. Philip Ney tells a story of a woman who came to him for counseling for her six-year-old child who was having nightmares, wetting the bed, and suffering from separation anxiety. Dr. Ney, in his interview with the mother, asked her about any pregnancy losses. She told him about two abortions that she had prior to giving birth to this child. Then in a separate interview with the child, Dr. Ney asked the child to draw a picture of her family. She was an only child, and yet she drew a picture with her

mom, dad, brother, sister, and herself. She had a sense of the missing siblings." – Excerpt from the book ***Recall Abortion*** [20]

Pennywise the Abortionist

The razor-like teeth of Pennywise the clown tearing off the arm of little Georgie can be seen as a powerful metaphor for the actions of an abortionist, especially in later-term procedures.

Former abortionist Dr. Anthony Levatino describes a D&E abortion:

> "… in a D&E procedure, you must use a grasping clamp…there's rows of teeth…When this gets a hold of something it does not let go…grabbing at parts of the baby, and then getting a hold and pulling, and you really pull…all of a sudden you pull out an arm or a leg that big and put it down on the table next to you…" [21]

The allure of the media and entertainment complex, the 24-hour news cycle, and our ever-present gadgets and devices, can keep us perpetually distracted. There has been a conspiracy of silence about the disappearance of close to 60 million children missing since abortion was legalized in 1973.

Our collective denial of this national tragedy prevents individuals and families from the necessary opportunity to repent, grieve and heal from the loss of our many fellow children, grandchildren, brothers and sisters, and nieces and nephews.

20 Morana, J. (January 24, 2013.) *Recall Abortion.* Saint Benedict Press

21 "See for Yourself" Gospel of Life Interview with Dr Anthony Levatino. https://www.priestsforlife.org/gospeloflife/see-for-yourself.htm

It brings to mind Bill's reaction to the missing, dismembered and murdered children in their town of Derry:

"Are we just going to pretend it didn't happen?"

Kevin Burke, LSW • Theresa Burke, Ph.D • Rev. Frank Pavone

CHAPTER FOUR

How Abortion Has Weakened Our "Cultural Immune System" and Prepared the Way for Transgender Madness

"A Virginia high-school teacher, Peter Vlaming, was fired in December 2018 after refusing to address a transgender student by the student's preferred pronoun." [22]

"But I don't want to go among mad people," Alice remarked. 'Oh, you can't help that," said the Cat: "we're all mad here...'
– Lewis Carroll, Alice in Wonderland

We know that under great stress, deprived of proper rest and nutrition, our immune systems are weakened. The immune response is compromised as it struggles to recognize and respond to threats. In this weakened state, we are more vulnerable to illness.

Can a nation of people have a type of collective immune system?

After 45 years of legalized abortion in the U.S., and close to 60 million procedures, there are few families that have

22 Dreher, R. (December 7, 2018). *Peter Vlaming Vs. Trans Tyrants.* American Conservative. TheAmericanConservative.com

not been directly impacted by the loss of a son or daughter, grandchild, sibling, nephew or niece.

Millions of our fellow citizens have been complicit in the death of an unborn child; e.g., paid for the procedure, pressured or encouraged abortion, drove a friend to the abortion center.

Thousands of medical and mental health professionals, educators, and politicians have participated directly in the death of the unborn.

This is a shared national trauma.

We know that individuals can suffer from depression, anxiety and other emotional and physical symptoms from traumatic loss. They are vulnerable to substance abuse and other forms of self-medication when they are denied the opportunity to work through their painful feelings and grieve their losses.

These symptoms can leave women and men vulnerable to having poor boundaries and to exhibit impulsive self-destructive behaviors for a time in their intimate relationships, especially in the aftermath of the abortion event.

What is the impact when an entire population of individuals, couples, and families suffer from a shared national trauma?

The continued unfolding of the *shockwaves of abortion* [23] has left our families and communities, especially minority neighborhoods with high abortion rates, and children with

23 The Silent No More Campaign launched in 2015 an initiative called "Healing the Shockwaves of Abortion," and it points out the multifaceted wounds abortion causes beyond the baby, mom and dad to the grandparents, siblings, other family members, friends, abortionists, and pro-life advocates. See www.AbortionShockwaves.com.

emotional challenges and learning disabilities, vulnerable to exploitation.

The Transgender Virus

The rapid advance of transgender activism in the last few years may be just one warning sign that our culture's immune system is seriously compromised. This activism has nothing to do with the respect which we all should acknowledge is to be extended to every human person in every circumstance.

Rather, it has to do with a radical minority, intent on re-designing traditional and universally accepted norms and convictions about gender and family. This minority and its ideology are assisted by powerful allies in entertainment and media, to infiltrate our communities and our schools.

Like the abortion rights revolutionaries, the transgendered movement is denying fundamental, physical realities of human existence, and they are prepared to lie, manipulate information and language, and viciously attack anyone that dares challenge their agenda. They are eager to exploit and mutilate our vulnerable children to advance their radical cause.

Like a compromised immune system, parents and educators, counselors and medical professionals find themselves, weak, defenseless, in denial of the threat, or promoting this madness.

Healthy Organs Were Amputated

Dr. Kathleen "Kelly" Levinstein, Ph.D., is a Professor of Social Work at the University of Michigan, Flint. Her research and advocacy work includes human and civil rights violations against the autistic community.

Dr. Levinstein shares a tragic and cautionary tale about the vulnerability of children with autism to the radical agenda of transgender activists. Dr. Levinstein has a daughter who has undergone transgender medical transition:

> "My daughter, who is on the autism spectrum -when she was 16, she began watching a TV show called "Degrassi," which featured a FtoM character. After a few weeks, she announced that she was not actually…lesbian, as she had previously said, but was in fact trans. She started attending a local PFLAG where she met many trans people, including a number of FtoM trans teenagers who were raving about a certain "gender therapist who gave my daughter the go-ahead to have a bilateral mastectomy after only two sessions…Healthy organs were amputated…
>
> It is a crime not just against women, but particularly against disabled women. So many of these young women who are "transitioning" are also autistic." [24]

Walt Heyer is an author and public speaker with a passion for mentoring individuals whose lives have been torn apart by unnecessary gender-change surgery. He shares in an article in the Federalist of a custody battle that features a mother taking her 6-year-old son down the dark road of gender transitioning that could lead to the boy's chemical castration at age 8.

The father says the boy acts fine with him and does not support this encouragement of the child transitioning. The mother took her ex-husband to court because he uses male pronouns when referring to the boy, (who the mother calls

24 Levinstein, K. (May 6, 2016). *Social Work Professor Speaks out on Behalf of her FtM Autistic Daughter.* 4thWaveNow. 4thWaveNow.com

Luna) and takes his son to the barber for haircuts...when his hair gets long.

Heyer shares:

> "Misdiagnosis of gender dysphoria happens around the world, and people's lives are harmed when it does... I wrote a book, "Trans Life Survivors," that shares many first-hand stories of misdiagnosis of gender dysphoria and the heart-breaking results." [25]

There is another movement that promotes the mutilation and medical experimentation on vulnerable children. Planned Parenthood harvests the healthy organs of unborn little boys and girls torn from the womb of their mothers.

More Cultural Chaos...or Recovery of Sanity?

Saint Teresa of Calcutta:

> *"The so-called right to abortion...has sown violence and discord at the heart of the most intimate human relationships...the greatest destroyer of peace today is abortion... your decision [to legalize abortion] has deformed a great nation."* [26]

The further we are removed from our moral and spiritual Judeo-Christian heritage, and the absolute providence of our Creator over human life, the further we travel with Alice down the rabbit hole into cultural chaos and madness.

We need to protect our young people from the radical

---

25 Heyer, W. (November 11, 2018).   *Mom Dresses Six-Year-Old Son As Girl, Threatens Dad With Losing His Son For Disagreeing.* The Federalist. TheFederalist. com

26 Mother Teresa's Letter to the US Supreme Court on Roe v. Wade. (February 1994).

transgender ideology. Like teacher Peter Vlaming, parents, educators, and community leaders need to firmly assert their freedom to speak and act in accordance with their beliefs, and to respectfully but firmly resist those who would redefine reality itself. Whatever the cost, we must find and impart the strength to effectively protect our vulnerable children.

An important step to restore sanity will be renewed commitment by our Churches, politicians, and citizens to heal our national trauma. We need to elect politicians that understand that abortion not only attacks the life of preborn children, but it is also eating away at the foundation of our society.

Many of our fellow citizens would benefit from abortion recovery programs. Women and men are strengthened as spouses and parents when they open up their hearts and souls to repentance and healing of this deep wound.

If we fail to confront the threats to our national immune system, we will see a nation that becomes increasingly irrational, divided, weak and vulnerable to internal and external attacks.

CHAPTER FIVE

Primal Fear:
Abortion and Adult Children of Divorce

When we think of the impact of divorce on children, there is often the assumption that if the parents work together in good faith, and do not place the children in the middle of their conflicts and relational drama, then in time the children will adjust and be fine.

Leila Miller is the editor of *"Primal Loss: The Now-Adult Children of Divorce Speak."* [27] Miller shares in an article entitled, *The Adult Children of Divorce Find Their Voice,* [28] that as she began the process of compiling research for her book she was shocked at the level of pain she encountered:

> "… I started asking adult children of divorce about their experiences. I eventually wrote up a brief questionnaire, appealing to social media for volunteers… I learned that not only does the pain of divorce continue into adulthood, but the suffering is not lessened even if the child experiences a "good divorce."

27 Miller, L. (May 20, 2017) *Primal Loss: The Now-Adult Children of Divorce Speak.* LCB Publishing; 1 edition

28 Miller, L. (July 17 2017). *The Adult Children of Divorce Find Their Voice.* The Institute for Family Studies. If.Studies.org

...A 50-year-old wife and mother whose parents shared custody and got along well after their divorce told me:

"I was devastated as a child when my dad drove away, and I will never forget standing in our front yard literally screaming, 'Come back!' I didn't understand what was happening, and my three-year-old sister certainly didn't understand...I would honestly say I 'survived' the divorce, but the fall-out wasn't pretty: Lots of acting out and 'unsettled' behavior. It really skewed the way I looked at guys and what I thought 'love' was. If marriage wasn't forever, why should anything else be?"

A 55-year-old woman shares her emotional experience of divorce:

"I believe [the divorce] instilled a fear of abandonment in me with regard to all of my relationships. I developed problems trusting people to be there for me, believing that when the going got rough, people would leave me. I never learned any skills for solving the conflict in relationships. As much as I desperately craved intimacy and love, the closer someone came to me, the more terrified I was of getting hurt, or worse—abandoned. I unconsciously sabotaged relationships, as I didn't know how to receive and accept real love..."

Abortion and Adult Children of Divorce

On Saturday morning of a Rachel's Vineyard abortion healing Weekend, participants share their abortion story. But they are encouraged to share that abortion event in the context of their overall life experiences. Their stories reveal that some children from divorced families can be overwhelmed by their emotions when facing an unplanned pregnancy, and in the aftermath of the abortion procedure.

Divorce can be such a seismic emotional event for some children, that when faced with an unplanned pregnancy later in life, they may panic and try to establish some sense of control as soon as possible – control they did not have as children.

They may have deep ambivalence about becoming a parent and terrified of losing their partner. While these feelings are common to others facing an unplanned pregnancy, with children of divorce, the level of anxiety and panic can be even more intense.

The aftermath of the abortion event is complicated grief for the children of divorce. It seems that there is a complex emotional dynamic at work here that touches on both the divorce and abortion events. It may be helpful to look at abortion and divorce in the context of one being both *victim* and *perpetrator*.

The experience of divorce can be like an *emotional abortion*. A child can have a sense of being violently separated from what was previously thought to be a stable and lifelong family unit. A child who was traumatized by the experience of divorce, and later participates in the death of their unborn child, magnifies an already deep and complex wound.

The adult child of divorce has the experience of being both innocent victim, and later a type of perpetrator, by participating in the abuse/death of their innocent unborn child. In other cases, a woman or man may feel pressured to have the abortion, overwhelmed by their emotions, or have no voice or say in the matter. These feelings of anxiety, panic, and powerlessness can reenact the emotional devastation of the divorce event.

The abortion experience may connect in a very toxic way

with that wounded inner child resulting in depression, anxiety, anger issues, sleep disturbance, increased drug and alcohol use, and acting out this complicated grief leading to problems in intimate relationships.

Building A Foundation of Healing and Peace

Abortion healing programs can create a foundation of peace at the heart of this deep and complex wound. As women and men find healthy ways to process their abortion-related pain and grieve their losses, they are reconnected in love with their aborted children. They have a safe place to share their childhood wounds and allow their own inner child to have a voice, to be consoled and move toward healing and peace.

Women and men who have experienced divorce and abortion may benefit from developing a relationship with a counselor so they can continue to build on that foundation of healing in their lives.

CHAPTER SIX

The Impact of Abortion on Poor Communities: Bridging the Gap Between Pro-Life and Social Justice Christians

Kelly Rosati is the vice president of Community Outreach at *Focus on the Family*:

"… it often seems as if pro-life and pro-justice Christians come from two different planets…They lean in different political directions, and each thinks the other should prioritize the issues differently…they have little interest in working together—and in fact, they can often seem "at odds" with one another." (*Christianity Today*, August 2015)

Public Religion Research Institute's 2012 American Values Survey[29], revealed the division between those who identify as *social justice* and *right to life* Catholics:

Social justice Catholics (60%): believe…the Catholic Church should focus more on social justice and the obligation to help the poor, even if it means focusing less on issues like abortion and the right to life.

29 Cox, D. et al. (October 22, 2012). *2012 Pre-Election American Values Survey.* Public Religion Research Institute. Prri.org

Right to life Catholics (31%): believe that the Catholic Church should focus more on abortion and the right to life in its statements about public policy, even if it means focusing less on issues like social justice and the obligation to help the poor."

Social justice Christians and public servants of all denominations and political parties fail to understand the dynamic connection that exists between abortion and the challenges faced by those suffering poverty and oppression. Pro-life advocacy, abortion prevention, and healing after abortion are essential in communities ravaged by violence, family breakdown, and social and economic injustice.

There are two populations served in abortion healing programs can help us better understand this relationship between abortion and poverty:

1. Minority female victims of sexual abuse and other trauma

2. The Male Prison Population

Sexual Abuse, Traumatic Re-Enactment, and Abortion

In *Forbidden Grief: The Unspoken Pain of Abortion*, Theresa Burke reveals that while abortion may initially appear to solve the problem of an unplanned pregnancy, the unfolding consequences of the procedure can be devastating for women with a previous history of sexual, emotional and physical abuse.

Dr. Burke shares in *Forbidden Grief* that the invasive and painful experience of the abortion procedure serves to re-enact the physical and emotional violation of previous sexual abuse and other trauma. After the abortion these women may experience a powerful resurgence of symptoms; addictions, impulsive acting out in relationships, episodes of rage, anxiety, depression, self-injury, nightmares, and difficulty sleeping.

The shockwaves of abortion have especially devastated the African American family in the United States.[30] Since 1973, 13 million African American pregnancies have been ended by abortion.

In spite of overall falling abortion rates in the U.S., numbers released in 2018 by the CDC revealed… abortion ratios actually increased among black women as compared to white women… nearly half of all pregnancies among black women end in abortion (472 per 1,000), while among white women only 16 percent of pregnancies are aborted (161 per 1,000). **In New York City, where Planned Parenthood is headquartered, more black babies are aborted than are born alive (1,180 abortions for every 1,000 live births).** [31]

If we look at the rate of sexual abuse among Africa Americans, we find a group of women that is especially vulnerable to post-abortion complications. Statistics reveal that 1 in 4 or 3.3 million African American women have been sexually abused.[32]

It is indeed challenging to face the scope and complexity of the problems facing poor families. But abortion creates emotional, spiritual and physical wounds and vulnerabilities

---

30 According to the Census Bureau, the rate of abortions in 2006 among black women was 50 per 1,000, compared with 14 for white women and 22 for "other" women.

31 Goldberg, A. (February 11 2019). *Abortion's Devastating Impact Upon Black Americans.* Public Discourse. ThePublicDiscourse.com

32 Stone, R. (March 8, 2005). *No Secrets No Lies: How Black Families Can Heal from Sexual Abuse.* Harmony.

that only exacerbate a woman's pre-existing trauma.

Women are left more vulnerable to ongoing exploitation, dysfunction, and abuse in their relationships. We know that this instability and dysfunction in relationships leads to a breakdown in family life, leaving women and their children vulnerable to predatory relatives, partners, and friends.

The cycle continues; more abuse, more trauma, more abortions, more death.

Abortion prevention and abortion healing – if possible after the initial abortion – is essential to help break dysfunctional patterns in the lives of the poor (including repeat abortions, which make up close to half of all procedures.)

The emotional and spiritual recovery process in abortion healing programs helps to significantly reduce destructive symptoms and behaviors and provide a foundation to build a healthier relationship with God, spouses/partners, and living children.

Abortion Healing and Prison Ministry – Reclaiming Lost Fatherhood

The Diocese of Palm Beach has a vibrant prison ministry at the maximum-security facilities in that area. Under the leadership of Catholic Charities and therapist Donna Gardner, they began ministering to men with abortion loss

in the prison population using a support group version of
Rachel's Vineyard along with exercises from the *Healing a
Father's Heart* bible study.

Initially, there was some understandable skepticism by prison
ministry staff of the need for such a program. What they
quickly learned is that close to 90% of the inmates were part
of abortion decisions in the past, and it did impact their lives
in powerful ways.

The healing journey of the inmates has revealed something
very important about the interaction of abortion with
childhood loss. This has relevance to men outside the prison
walls in our poorest communities who have been hurt by
abusive or absent fathers; and those families where children
were emotionally wounded when their parents divorced.

Here's some of what these men have taught us:

> – The abortion healing journey provides a unique
> opportunity for those men who have unresolved rage
> and hurt from fathers who were absent and/or abusive, a
> common wound of many of the prisoners. Many inmates
> had fathers that failed to treasure them as sons and serve
> as good models of manhood/fatherhood. You can think
> of this rejection as a type of *emotional abortion*.

> – A solid post-abortion healing program allows the
> participant to progress through the steps of emotional
> and spiritual recovery so they can repent of their role in
> the child's death and restore their fatherly relationship
> with the aborted child or children.

> – They invite the Holy Spirit into the dark wounds of
> their own father loss, abuse, or neglect. As they address
> their abortion wounds men learn on a deep and intimate

level *how to grieve*, within a process immersed in God's Word, the sacraments, and the Holy Spirit.

– The abortion recovery experience empowers them to let go of the rage and unhealthy behaviors that were their only way of coping with their pain in the past. They are restored and strengthened as men and fathers.

For Christians to emphasize the foundational primacy of the right to life of the unborn in no way diminishes the value of ministry to the poor, sick, elderly, and disabled. A society that protects its most vulnerable members and treasures the dignity of unborn children will be even more effective in building a just and compassionate church and society.

African Americans and Abortion Loss
By David Williams

To understand the unique vulnerability of the African American community to abortion, we need to look at how traumatic slavery was for the black family. Families were systematically and cruelly dismantled according to the business needs of the slavers. Men would be torn from their wives and children. They were bred like animals to create the optimal labor value for the slave businesses. Women were routinely sexually abused, raped and separated from their children. Many mothers would abort their unborn children rather than have them born into slavery.

African Americans were not looked at as human beings created in the image of God but something less than that. Because of this, they were seen as nothing more than property to be done with however their 'masters' saw fit. This sinful, ungodly system of slavery, which lasted for over 200 years in our nation, I believe not only oppressed, devalued and traumatized African Americans but also ingrained in us certain mindsets about marriage, family, sex and abortion.

Now in our nation, babies in the womb, who are created in the image of God, are viewed as less than human. They are seen as nothing more than the property of the woman, who happens to be a mother, to be kept or discarded according to her choice. This is very similar to the way that African Americans were viewed during slavery.

Even though laws in our nation have changed that have freed and given equal rights to African Americans the mindset among some that blacks are inferior (racism) is still alive and well. When you combine these facts it does not surprise me that the majority of abortion providers are in urban centers and that over 30% of abortions are by black women (though they comprise only 13% of women).

The abortion industry and their allies think the solution for the high rate of out of wedlock pregnancies and other social problems in poor minority communities is abortion and more birth control. What they fail to see, or ignore is that this attacks us in those areas of historical traumatic vulnerability. Those that have a previous history of trauma are more likely to experience more serious post-abortion reactions such as debilitating anxiety/depression, substance abuse and/or to act out their grief and pain in dysfunctional relationships. Obviously, this feeds the very problems the pro-abortion forces say they are rescuing us from. But the truth is, we are being exploited and targeted in a very direct way by the abortion industry.

I often have an opportunity to share about my own abortion loss and healing in my speaking ministry. I am finding more and more that this opens up the door for pastors and other church leaders, educators and laymen to share about their own shame, guilt, and pain from being involved in an abortion decision.

I recently spoke with a church leader who had an abortion with his wife over 20 years ago. They were never able to have children. This is a very deep wound. After sharing with him he expressed an interest in getting connected to a group for healing at a Pregnancy Resource Center. I am finding that his response is rare. Most Pastors, church, and ministry leaders that I speak with are reluctant to go through a healing program and to be public in any way about this secret in their past.

As men, we can all struggle with the sin of pride. We understandably want to appear together, strong and in control. It's hard for men who are used to being looked up to as morally sound, virtuous and holy men and church leaders to let their guard down and open up this wound to deeper healing…let alone publicly share such a shameful secret.

Until you receive the grace from God to put aside that pride, that fear of losing control, fear of the powerful feelings associated with abortion loss, you naturally "don't want to go there."

I believe that as long as we live with these secrets while acting as if all is well, then we miss out on experiencing the healing grace and forgiveness of Christ. I think that this circumvents our ability to freely and fully minister God's word to others. The thought becomes "who am I to speak up about abortion when I also am guilty and wounded by it." This keeps too many silenced. Thus abortion continues to ravage lives in the African American community and leave in its wake multitudes of broken women and men who sit in church feeling guilty, condemned and afraid to confess what they've done and seek healing.

The fullness of the gospel message is compromised when our leaders fail to address this issue in their own lives. It communicates that "my position, image, and ego are more important than letting Christ take full possession of my life"...especially those areas that are most shrouded in secrecy and shame.

But when you don't do the grief and healing work around that loss, this can lead to acting-out and ministry burn out. Equally important, by not dealing with these vulnerable wounds, we leave ourselves open to the exploitation of these emotional vulnerabilities by Satan. Secret wounds can feed secret acting out of unresolved emotional pain, grief, guilt, and anger from abortion; pornography viewing, extra-marital affairs, workaholic tendencies, anger issues, and health problems can all be at least in part related to an unresolved abortion loss.

Jesus is telling us to put aside our pride, our privilege and our positions for a time and learn to open ourselves fully to his grace and Lordship of our lives. I can tell you from personal experience, you will be richly blessed. You will come to more fully realize the will of Christ in your life.

If you are a minister/pastor or another church leader, you will be freed to preach the Gospel of Life and the Gospel of the healing power of Jesus over abortion wounds. You will have the privilege of being used by God to lead others to forgiveness, healing, and hope. Your ministry will be empowered and blessed in ways that you could never imagine prior to taking that step.

For a number of years, I have frequently shared parts of my story with teens and college students. Though I would mention the abortion that my girlfriend had when I was 19 I had no idea of how deeply I was wounded by it. In 2013, I was asked to share about the abortion experience at a Pregnancy Resource Center banquet in Cincinnati, Ohio where Brad Mattes of *Life Issues* was in attendance.

A few days after the event Brad and I had a phone conversation where he asked me a question which at the time I thought was weird. He said to me, "David how have you invited Jesus to heal you from the effects of your past abortion?" My initial thoughts were…*I am ok that was so long ago (22 years) and I have been a Christian for 16 years.* But I said to him "I have not specifically done anything to heal from the wounds of the abortion."

He then asked me if he could send me a book *Fatherhood Aborted* and if I would be interested in going through a post-abortion Bible study with a male peer counselor. I told him that I would be open to both. As I read the book and went through the bible study I began to see the effects and the deep hurt of the abortion in my life both prior to and after coming to know Jesus. I would have never made the connection.

As I went through the bible study, I began and continue to experience God's forgiveness, grace, and healing in ever-increasing measure. It has impacted my relationship with my wife, children, and ministry in ways far beyond anything I could have imagined. By God's grace, He has called me to be a champion for the unborn, to minister to those in the midst of a crisis and broken by past abortion. (Genesis50:20)

[David lives in Orlando with his wife and their four children. He also has a son who lives in Pittsburgh and a daughter Miriam who he looks forward to meeting in heaven. David worked for 10 years with Cru, formerly Campus Crusade for Christ, ministering to college students in Northeast Ohio, serving as a traveling speaker and also as a chaplain for one

season with the Cincinnati Bengals. In 2013, David decided to devote more time to his God-given passion to preach. Along with speaking, David mentors college students and ministers with Pregnancy Resource Centers to be a voice for the unborn and mentor men who have been affected by or whose partners are considering abortion.]

David Williams Contact Information:

Website: www.davidwilliamsspeaks.com
Email: davidwilliamsspeaks@gmail.com

Kevin Burke, LSW • Theresa Burke, Ph.D • Rev. Frank Pavone

CHAPTER SEVEN

Fetal Disability Abortions –
Compassionate Choice?

Every year in the United States thousands of pregnant mothers will undergo routine pre-natal tests and receive what is called a "poor prenatal diagnosis." This means that their baby is afflicted with a chromosomal abnormality or a serious defect in a vital organ.

With the increase in genetic testing and fertility treatments more couples are facing these difficult decisions. Parents are often pressured by doctors, therapists, friends, and family to "terminate" the pregnancy. They are given the grim prospect of a child born prematurely who will die shortly after birth or suffer severe deformities and a brief life filled with suffering and pain.

Couples are vulnerable when confronted with many levels of anxiety, uncertainty, and fear that are natural when trying to process such an event. Sadly, health care professionals, friends, and family feed their worst fears. Often with the best of intentions, they fail to offer life-affirming alternatives that respect the dignity of unborn life, and in the long run, are in the best interest of the mother and father, and especially their relationship.

Most couples only receive *non-directive counseling*, which means they are told only the various challenges and likely prognosis of the condition without offering other life-affirming resources. This can be overwhelming and lead the parents in the aftershock of this news to see abortion as the best solution.

In one study, 80% of parents who received 'non-directive' counseling chose to abort while 80% of parents who were provided with the option of perinatal palliative care chose to carry their child to term. [33]

Tragically, more than 90 percent of these pregnancies end in abortion. When abortion is the preferred course of "treatment" not only is the baby's life ended, but the lives of these parents are changed forever. Like our first parents in the Garden of Eden, assuming this power over life and death has far-reaching consequences beyond the decision to abort. The fallout from this loss places a tremendous strain on a couple as they struggle to come to terms with the shock and pain of their experience.

Research confirms that women suffer years after the procedure:

> Women 2-7 years after were expected to show a significantly lower degree of traumatic experience and grief than women 14 days after termination...Contrary to the hypothesis, however, the results showed no significant inter-group differences.[34]

33 *A New Service for a New Era: Perinatal Palliative Care.*   Perspectives: The Newsletter of the DeVeber Institute for Bioethics and Social Research, Autumn 2008. DeVeber.org

34 Saunders, P. (October 17 2013). *Psychological Trauma after Abortion for Fetal Disability – Parents Need to Know the Facts.* Life Site News. LifeSiteNews.com

Complicated Grief

These parents suffer from a particularly complex form of grief and guilt. They hunger desperately for healing and peace but struggle to come to terms with their responsibility in the death of their child and the need for repentance, reconciliation, and healing. They feel strongly that their situation is "different" from others who abort.

Couples cling desperately to the idea that they did what was best for their child, saving them from life, however brief, of suffering and pain. In other scenarios, they must choose among healthier embryos or multiple fetuses so that the healthiest survive. Given the medical advice and pressure from a spouse or others, they feel they did not have a real choice. As with any abortion decision when women or men are feeling pressured in any way, or are ambivalent about their decision, they are at high risk for symptoms of emotional trauma.

The husband may see the abortion as protecting his wife from the pain of giving birth to a child who would have died, would die shortly after birth, or born with a physical and mental handicap that would present a burden to his wife and family. In their efforts to establish control and take action, men are tempted to see abortion as the best solution.

After the abortion, there can be considerable anger at God, whom couples often blame for putting them in this situation. One couple expresses this struggle:

> "If we were given a normal child, we would not be suffering like this. We are different from others who have aborted because we wanted this child. God put us in this impossible situation, forcing us to make these painful decisions. We are left without our child, and with

Kevin Burke, LSW • Theresa Burke, Ph.D • Rev. Frank Pavone

powerful feelings of confusion, resentment anger and grief."

Without a healing process for this complicated grief, this pain will surely impact marital intimacy, communication and trust and the relationship of parents with their living children.

Empty Arms and Wounded Hearts

When the rationalization and the seemingly wise counsel of doctors and others fade away after the abortion, a mother and father are faced with empty arms and a wounded heart. They must accept the painful realization that this decision also aborted their opportunity to hold this child, and offer their son or daughter love and affection for however long the baby lived. In the case of Down's Syndrome and other conditions, they were given a child with special challenges to love and care for, and in their rejection of that child, something in them has also died both individually and as a couple.

It is only when these mothers and fathers come to a clearer and honest understanding of their abortion loss that they can begin to repent, grieve and heal. The healing process can never be forced. We must be patient, especially in the early stages of healing as the wound is very raw. There can initially be great defensiveness. It's important to acknowledge their pain and loss, the confusing nature of the decisions and challenges that their fertility treatment/testing and medical care presented to them.

However, at some point in the process, when they are ready and with God's grace and much prayer, they can face the truth that their abortion decision led them to make a choice that violated their parental hearts, created to love any children they conceived regardless of the challenges.

They come to see that the abortion was a crisis of faith, one that we all face at different times in our lives when we fail to trust God, and we make decisions that violate His will for us. We must always speak to them in love, as fellow sinners who have aborted God's will in our lives.

Lord, Please Help Me Not to Be So Perfect

Susan attended a Rachel's Vineyard Weekend Retreat after aborting a child diagnosed with a condition that would lead to her daughter's death shortly after birth. She expressed a desire to leave the retreat Saturday morning.

Susan shared:

> "I don't fit in with these other women and men who freely chose abortion for selfish reasons. I had no choice. The choice I made was in the best interests of my child."

The minister serving on the retreat team spoke with her after breakfast on Saturday encouraging her to stay through the afternoon and then if she still felt the same way, she could leave. Because of her trust in this priest, and the help of the Holy Spirit she decided to stay.

A major breakthrough occurred for Susan following the Living Scripture Exercise of the *Woman Healed of a Hemorrhage* offered on Saturday afternoon. In this exercise, the participants have an opportunity to touch a cloth representing the cloak of Christ.

Susan approached the cloak that flowed from the base of a wooden cross and prayed:

> "Lord, please help me not to be so perfect, to want everything in my life to be perfect...even my child."

She broke down in tears as she shared these beautiful words of repentance and grace. She continued on the weekend receiving an incredible amount of healing and peace. At the memorial service Susan read a letter to her child apologizing for not having the courage to go through with the child's birth and imminent death:

Our Dearest Marie,

How are you, sweetie? How are you doing in Heaven? Mommy and daddy really miss you. Your brother, Vincent, asks about you all the time....Your sister, Veronica, would have loved to have a little sister like you because you and she would have been best friends...You are our little angel, our most beautiful child.

But we are both so sorry that we denied you that chance to be with our family. You would have loved to be with us, to hear our voices, to have us touch you, hold you, and kiss you. Even though it may only have been a short time: months, days, or maybe just hours, deep down I know that it would have been worth it. We would have learned so much from you: how to love, how to serve, how to be humble, and how to trust in our God completely!

Dearest Marie... Your daddy and I both need your prayers. I know that you are in good hands, as Jesus has shown me that Mother Mary is taking care of you. We will not worry about you, but you are forever in our hearts. We love you so much, with all our hearts and all our souls. We promise that we will pray to you always, tell you about all that is going on in our family.

We thank God that He has blessed us with you, that He has given us a chance to come to this retreat so that both your daddy and I would feel closer to you. We look forward to the day that we will meet in Heaven, in the eternal home of God our Father, where we can finally hold you close and give you hugs and kisses.

Thank you for forgiving us. You are forever our child and we are so blessed to be your parents.

Love always,

Mommy and Daddy

It may take longer to make this type of transition and conversion but if they are open to an abortion healing program, individuals will experience some release of their pain and anguish. They may still struggle to fully embrace repentance and healing. The couple may remain attached to the idea that "we did what was in the best interests of our child" and may still wrestle with feelings of anger and resentment.

Offer ongoing support and share any after-care services that might assist them. Let them know that the grace of their healing experience has planted seeds, and in time they will bear greater fruit.

For those offering healing programs, it is important when couples register for the weekend, that you give them a good overview of your healing process. With that understanding, we can entrust them to the God of mercy and pray for the Holy Spirit to open their hearts to his forgiveness and healing, according to His perfect will and time.

Perinatal Hospice

Those ministering to engaged or married couples are in an excellent position to offer alternatives to abortion when a couple receives the painful news there is a problem with their pregnancy. The type of counseling couples receive is critical to the decision to abort or give birth to a disabled child.

Fortunately, there is a growing movement to provide *Perinatal Hospice* **www.perinatalhospice.org** that supports couples who journey through the difficult birth, death, and funeral of their child. With encouragement and education, they help provide the vital healing experience of embracing their child with love for as long as the baby lives.

Though deeply painful, it gives parents and families the opportunity to celebrate the child's life and to grieve this loss in a healthy way. The couple and their family experience the natural process of grief. With the support team of doctors, nurses, chaplains and social workers they can find healing and meaning in their suffering and loss.

Abortion robs parents of this opportunity. While we can struggle to understand the meaning of suffering and death, especially of an infant, God's grace and blessing abound when life is embraced, loved and released with dignity.

For those with a Down Syndrome diagnosis, we must provide opportunities for parents to learn of the blessings as well as the real challenges that these children will present, to counter the negative picture presented by proponents of abortion.

It may be beneficial to have some contacts of parents who have a Down Syndrome child who would be willing to speak to those faced with a Down Syndrome diagnosis. Once parents get over the initial shock and fear of the unknown, their lives are filled with peace and as one mother told us, "I live with pure joy every day. I'm learning about unconditional love from my son."

Resources:

Prenatal Partners for Life

www.prenatalpartnersforlife.org

From their website: "If you have come to this site because you or someone you know has received an adverse or negative prenatal diagnosis, you have come to the right place. We are parents who have gone through similar circumstances and we want to offer support. We are here to help you. You are not alone!"

https://www.youtube.com/watch?v=PdrLKGmM-pc&feature=emb_logo

This is a beautiful YouTube Video. From the video description: "John Paul Johnson lived for seventeen minutes after birth, surrounded by his family and those who loved him. He was theirs for a time: and every moment of his life in the womb and after birth was celebrated by his family. His mother, Clíona, talks about those precious moments with John Paul, and the love he brought to everyone." See more at **http://www.everylifecounts.ie**

Kevin Burke, LSW • Theresa Burke, Ph.D • Rev. Frank Pavone

CHAPTER EIGHT

The Apostle and the Revolutionary

By Kevin Burke, LSW

In my book **Tears of the Fisherman** [35], I explore in depth how men are wounded by their role in the death of children in the womb, and the challenges of facing, grieving and healing this loss.

You may wonder why it is important to focus on men's experience of abortion loss and other trauma. Why should our society be concerned about the millions of men, some with past abuse and other trauma in their histories, involved in abortion decisions and procedures?

The Apostle Simon Peter and the communist revolutionary Vladimir Lenin were men separated by thousands of years of history. Yet both experienced a life-changing traumatic event in their lives. How they responded to and processed their grief and emotional pain would change the world in very different ways.

Most men who have experienced abortion loss will not go on have such a dramatic impact on the larger world as Peter and Lenin. But as we learned in processing the abortion history of male prisoners, how men process a traumatic loss

---

35 Burke, K. (2017) *Tears of the Fisherman.* PFL Publishing.

does impact their lives, relationships, and communities in significant ways.

Simon Bar Jonah, Inc.

Prior to meeting Jesus of Nazareth, Simon Peter worked in a family business in the important regional fishing industry on the Sea of Galilee. When Peter responded to the call of Jesus, he likely turned over his responsibilities to a relative, and was now a "fisher of men." Jesus later appointed him the leader of His community of believers.

As the Apostles gathered for what would be their final Passover meal together, Jesus turned to Peter, and with great love and urgency said:

> "Simon, Simon, behold, Satan has demanded permission to sift you like wheat; but I have prayed for you, that your faith may not fail; and you, when once you have turned again, strengthen your brothers." (Luke 22: 31-32)

Peter made a bold proclamation to re-establish the integrity of his leadership among the other apostles and his unquestioned fidelity to Jesus:

> … "Lord, I am ready to go with you to both prison and to death!" (Luke 22:33)

Just a few short hours later all hell was breaking loose. Under the cover of darkness, Jesus was arrested, beaten and abused by Temple guards, and facing Roman torture and execution. Peter rightly feared that as the designated leader of the Twelve Apostles he might suffer the same fate. Isolated and afraid, Peter three times publicly denied any association with Jesus.

As the first light of dawn appeared on the horizon, Peter remembered the prophetic warning of his Master at the Last Supper. He was ashamed and cried bitter tears of remorse as

Jesus was condemned to suffer the horrific torture of Roman scourging and crucifixion.

Many Years Later…

A seminal event in the development of Vladimir Lenin as an icon of the communist revolution occurred many years before the Bolsheviks seized power in October 1917. This family trauma occurred shortly after the sudden death of Lenin's father in 1886.

Tsarist Russia at this time was plagued by inept leadership and a system of government that made it challenging for the nation to evolve and adapt in a rapidly changing world. Idealistic young men who hungered for greater economic development and intellectual freedom had no creative outlet for their passion. Radical leaders seduced youth into embracing terrorism and assassination to advance their cause.

Lenin's older brother Alexander was one such disenchanted, radicalized youth. On May 4, 1887, Alexander and his four companions, all in their twenties, were arrested after an unsuccessful attempt to assassinate the tsar. Despite his mother's pleas for mercy, on May 8 Alexander and his accomplices were executed.

How did the 17-year-old Vladimir react to the news of his brother's death? A close friend said, "I saw [his] deep grief but also his determination not to show it…"

After the execution of Alexander, Lenin's family was shunned by the bourgeois middle class of their hometown of Simbirsk. Town dignitaries who had attended their father's funeral, and longstanding friends, now rejected and abandoned the family.

Author Victor Sebestyen writes how Lenin's repressed grief, and the family's painful rejection, metastasized into a seething rage directed at the middle classes:

> This triggered the vitriolic, sometimes uncontrollable, loathing for 'liberals and middle-class do-gooders' that would henceforth show until his dying day. "The bourgeois... they will always be traitors and cowards," he declared with monotonous frequency from now onwards...A young boy who rarely thought about politics became radicalized almost overnight. [36]

Divergent Paths of Grief

Imagine if St. Peter had responded like Lenin to his traumatic loss. He might have channeled the powerful emotional energy generated by his shame and grief into acts of revenge and terror against the Temple's leadership and Roman forces of occupation. If Peter had chosen this path, he would have destroyed his vocation in Christ and brought the fury of Rome to crush the Church in her infancy.

After the resurrection, on the shores of the Sea of Galilee where Peter was first called to his special vocation as a "fisher of men," Jesus revealed another way.

Jesus created an opportunity for Peter to enter into the shame and grief of his three denials, to allow that toxic pain to surface so that their relationship could be restored within His merciful and healing embrace:

> Jesus asked Peter a third time, "Simon son of John, do you love me?" Peter was deeply hurt that Jesus had asked him a third time, "Do you love me?" "Lord, you know all things;" he replied, "You know I love you." Jesus said to him, "Feed My sheep. (John 21:17)

It is likely that during this exchange, Peter once again

36 Sebestyen, V. (November 7, 2017). *Lenin: The Man, the Dictator, and the Master of Terror.* Pantheon.

wept. But these tears flowed from healthy grieving, tears of cleansing and restoration. Peter could now be entrusted with pastoral authority in the Kingdom of God. This was an authority rooted in the deepest humility.

Men who attend abortion healing bible studies and retreats experience this mercy, transformation, and restoration by opening their hearts and souls to a healthy experience of reconciliation and grieving their lost fatherhood.

What If Lenin Followed Jesus...Instead of Revolution?

Lenin channeled the powerful emotional pain from the loss of his brother, and the rejection of his family, into a passion for revenge. The ideology of communism and class warfare provided the perfect vehicle for his toxic rage.

Imagine what a different course Russian and world history would have taken if Lenin chose the way of humility and faith, and like Peter, poured out his heart to Jesus?

A spiritual and emotional path of healing, perhaps with a holy orthodox priest or layman, would have provided a sacred space to share his pain. Such an experience may have helped the young Lenin see the grave threat to his immortal soul and the potential for greater evil that would flow from his obsession with revenge through the communist revolution.

Lenin might have devoted his life to helping Russia find a way forward in social and economic progress; a vision that respected what was best in her history, including the great spiritual heritage of the Russian Orthodox faith.

Instead, the politicized, weaponized rage of Lenin cast a dark and murderous shadow on the 20th century. Communism has been directly responsible for the death of 100 million people worldwide since the Russian Revolution of 1917. [37]

---

37 Rummel, R.J. (February 1, 1997) *Death by Government.* Routledge. [Rummel's research reveals that 110 million people, foreign and domestic, were killed by communist regimes from 1900 to 1987.]

SECTION II

OCEANS OF MERCY

*"Therefore, since we have a great high priest who has passed
through the heavens, Jesus, the Son of God, let us hold fast to
our confession. For we do not have a high priest who is unable
to sympathize with our weaknesses, but one who has similarly
been tested in every way, yet without sin. So let us confidently
approach the throne of grace to receive mercy and to find grace
for timely help."*

– Hebrews 4:14-16

Kevin Burke, LSW • Theresa Burke, Ph.D • Rev. Frank Pavone

CHAPTER NINE

Breaking the Silence / The Genesis of Rachel's Vineyard

By Kevin Burke, LSW

I attended an ecumenical training seminar for clergy and pastoral staff held in a northeast city. The subject of abortion came up in an informal discussion among some of the participants. A few people shared their frustration that we rarely hear the subject addressed from the pulpit.

A local Christian Pastor abruptly interjected; "Abortion is a private and sensitive issue. Whatever your position on abortion, Sunday services are not the place to talk about it. We can't let contentious and divisive politics enter our worship space."

I later had the opportunity to speak privately to this Pastor and share of my work as a counseling professional with women and men hurting after abortion. I agreed that the pulpit is no place to advocate for candidates or political parties. But I asked him to consider that many women and men in his congregation have experienced abortion, or have been closely associated with the abortion of a partner, friend, or family member.

I went on to ask, "Pastor, what does the silence of the

church communicate to those who are suffering emotional and spiritual pain related to a past abortion, and would benefit from a healing program? What does this silence communicate to a woman or man that is considering abortion during a difficult pregnancy situation?"

I shared briefly some of the common themes reflected in the abortion stories shared on our healing retreats. His response, "I never really thought about it that way."

The Pastor is not alone.

The silence in our churches sends the following very clear messages to those attending weekly services:

- We can't help you reconcile and come to peace with this painful part of your past, even if it's an obstacle to a closer relationship with God.

- It's best to deny and repress any painful feelings and memories about your abortion losses.

This is not only a problem in our churches.

The majority of professionals in psychology/psychiatry, medicine and education support "reproductive rights" and would not hesitate to counsel one of their patients or students to consider abortion when facing an unplanned or complicated pregnancy situation.

Many of our friends, family members, and co-workers are ambivalent about the issue and are easily turned off by the polarized, and seemingly intractable conflicts between the different sides. Others strongly support the continued legalization and easy access to abortion services.

Yet, the majority of these professionals and our fellow citizens have little understanding of what life is like for women and men after their abortion. Given the suppression of honest narratives about abortion in our media, entertainment and educational institutions, the public can remain insulated from the truth.

They may never hear of how this loss can impact the emotional and physical health, relationships, marriages and family life of those that experience the procedure or are complicit in other direct ways in the death of the unborn. Even those wounded by their past abortion experiences may prefer silence to facing this shadowy event from their past.

Yet, there is a great price to pay for this silence.

The Price of Silence and Denial

Leslie suffered for many years with times of depression, anxiety, and nightmares connected to her two abortions at age 16 and 19. She medicated her pain with alcohol, and later when married, she was involved in a number of shameful and secret extramarital affairs.

Later Leslie was given prescription drugs prescribed by her family doctor to treat depression, anxiety, and insomnia. None of the therapists, clergy/ministers or medical professionals she turned to for help asked her if she had a history of abortion and other pregnancy losses.

But what really hurt and angered Leslie was the failure of her spiritual leaders to recognize this hidden pain:

"If I had heard a compassionate and hope-filled message from my pastor, if I heard after my first abortion that there were healing programs available for people like me, I may have been able to prevent the death of my second child and get the help I needed much earlier in my life. I may have been able to save my husband and my children from living for years with the symptoms of this wound that was festering in my heart and soul…"

The Genesis of Rachel's Vineyard

By Theresa Burke

"I am the true vine, and my Father is the vine grower. He removes every branch in me that bears no fruit. Every branch that bears fruit he prunes to make it bear more fruit. You have already been cleansed by the word that I have spoken to you. Abide in me as I abide in you. Just as the branch cannot bear fruit by itself unless it abides in the vine, neither can you unless you abide in me."
– John 15: 1-5

Beginning in 1986 Theresa Burke developed the support group and weekend retreat models of Rachel's Vineyard. As she began to counsel those who lost children to abortion, she found that her clients benefitted greatly by gathering with others who had suffered this same loss. She also discovered that abortion loss required an integrated emotional and spiritual process to bring a deeper peace and healing to those suffering after abortion.

There are now close to 500 Rachel's Vineyard Retreat Sites offering over 1000 retreats a year in 70 countries around the world. There are both Catholic and Interdenominational formats. The program has been translated into 22 languages with more in progress.

An Overview of the Rachel's Vineyard Weekend

Participants gather with others who share this unique experience of loss, in an atmosphere of love, acceptance, and safety. This program utilizes some of key "steps of healing" found in programs like **Project Rachel**, but in a process where the stages of healing are incorporated into a weekend spiritual journey:

– At the heart of the retreat experience are creative and unique Living Scripture exercises that re-enact gospel passages where participants experience an intimate encounter with Christ. The soul is invited to speak its pain to Christ, who is present through the Word of God. There are no lectures, talks or teachings. It is an *"experience"* of God in the context of one's suffering and grief.

– Rachel's Vineyard is an integrated psychological and spiritual approach. The meditation, calming music, and prayer stimulate the frontal cortex, the part of the brain that integrates cognitive and emotional experiences. Without integrating these elements victims of trauma are left either in states of hyper-arousal and panic or dissociated, numb, and disconnected from their emotions. Activities and exercises are uniquely developed to provide a comforting yet at the same time cathartic step-by-step process that engages the senses and allows individuals to safely progress through the stages of grief after abortion.

– Daily Mass, Eucharistic Adoration, and the Sacrament of Reconciliation on Saturday evening of the Catholic Retreats.

– The retreat is facilitated by a team consisting of site leader, clergy/minister, counselor, and women and men who have experienced abortion and made the healing journey. Volunteers, (often past retreatants) offer confidential prayer support and Eucharistic adoration behind the scenes providing spiritual protection and empowering the healing work of the weekend.

The theological framework for the retreat is the *paschal mystery* of one's life. Retreat participants unite their own suffering to Christ's which began on Good Friday. They come to recognize the death caused by sin in their lives and grieve the death of the aborted children. As the pain and death are united with the person and mission of Jesus. By Sunday they share in the resurrection from the death caused by sin.

Blind Bartimaeus

The retreat begins Friday afternoon or evening with a *Living Scripture* about blind Bartimaeus: The scripture is read followed by a meditation where all are invited to imagine themselves like the blind man. Following the meditation, facilitators go to each person, calling them by name as they say:

"Take Courage he is calling you."

The participant responds: *"Jesus, son of David, have pity on me."*

The priest places his hand on their head and asks the question: *"What do you want me to do for you?"*

All are invited to make their response to the Lord. The honesty and desperation expressed in this first exercise set the tone for the work that follows. Jesus does not impose himself on us – he waits to be invited. He respects our boundaries and allows us to decide what it is we search for.

This is a vital step in the process: our recognition that we want help, are willing to ask for it and begin to open our hearts to the light of Christ.

After everyone has spoken, each person receives a candle to represent the light of Christ. We pray that this candle would illuminate our way into deep memories and emotions that we have forgotten or tried to hide. We ask for courage, strength and the truth.

Each *Living Scripture* exercise is followed with discussion questions and sharing. Each reflection ends with a closing prayer and a ritual to further help participants comprehend and feel the words of God being planted in their hearts.

Is There Anyone Here to Condemn You?

The next *Living Scripture* meditation is the woman caught in adultery. This exercise gives the women and men an opportunity to observe the mercy and compassion of Christ who sent away the accusers. They also reflect on the condemnation and judgments they have experienced from others and themselves.

We repeat the dialogue as we pass a large rock around the room from person to person asking the same question Jesus asked the woman caught in adultery:

"Is there anyone here to condemn you?" "Go and sin no more."

Many people know God forgives, but they just cannot forgive themselves. This seems to be one of the most common struggles. The bitterness and guilt is the only way they have known to remember their lost child. In the exercise that follows this meditation, participants are invited to pick up a rock and carry it with them throughout the weekend, to represent the burden of not being able to forgive themselves or others. As the weekend progresses, they have a very tangible reminder of the ways that unforgiveness is interfering with their lives and actions. They feel compassion for others who struggle to carry the rock and begin to perceive self-loathing, self-condemnation and anger in a different way.

The processing of these emotions through *Living Scripture* and the retreat rituals begins to release painful emotions, create new insights, and make room for a healthy expression of grief and later in the retreat, a more loving and healthy way to embrace and honor their unborn child that will not demand a living memorial of self-destruction or self-hatred.

The Cup of Bitterness

Before the closing on Friday evening, we pass *The Cup of Bitterness*. Each person names the feelings of guilt, shame, grief and self-hatred as they pour non-alcoholic wine into the cup. This passing of the cup is filled with all the distressing and bitter feelings carried by each person present. We pass the cup around again, this time drinking from the Cup of Bitterness, signifying our willingness to share in each other's secret suffering. The cup symbolizes the cup of bitterness shared before the great Exodus when Moses led God's people out from captivity. The first night of the retreat marks the end of slavery caused by sin and the entry into the freedom Jesus offers through forgiveness and redemption.

Sharing our Stories

On Saturday morning of the Rachel's Vineyard Retreat, participants share the story of their lives. Abortion can be a symptom of other hurts and losses; absent fathers, painful relationships with mothers, or problems that made abortion seem reasonable since many wanted to protect themselves from more hurt and abandonment. Telling one's story is an opportunity to open all wounds before the light of Christ.

In our experience, commonly half of those who attend Rachel's Vineyard have histories of molestation or some form of sexual abuse. The abortion itself can be a way they continue to re-enact trauma, acting out conflicts with the wounded inner child of rejection, shame, secrets, and further violation. The abortionist's hand or instrument can be experienced as an intimate and disturbing violation. The womb...after abortion becomes a tomb, and life is ended through this intrusion.

The Tomb of Lazarus

When the stories are finished the group re-enacts the story of Lazarus. Participants are anointed and symbolically bound for burial – naming the parts of themselves which have died because of sin. This ritual makes the visible the wounds which have been invisible. Participants asked to have their eyes wrapped if they have lost sight of God or their own goodness. They might request that their heart be wrapped with a gauze bandage, to symbolize a broken and fractured heart. They might request their feet to be wrapped if they have felt stuck in life, incapable of moving forward. A couple may request that their wedding ring hand be wrapped to demonstrate the symbolic death of their marriage that followed abortion.

Once everyone has named the parts of themselves that have died, two facilitators take the place of Martha and Mary who begin to grieve:

"Lord, if you had been here, our brothers and sisters would

not have died! If they had not lost sight of you, their children would not have died!"

In this exercise, they express their dismay as the Lord joins them in grief. This *Living Scripture* exercise gives everyone an opportunity to recognize that God weeps with them. He is the God of Life and he came that we might have life – yet as he looks upon all the signs of death before him now wrapped in burial cloths, he weeps. This exercise reveals the consolation of the Lord as words of life are spoken by the priest, who stands in the place of Christ, revealing the broken heart of God who shares in their suffering. They discover that this is a God that looks upon his children with love and compassion and longs to restore and redeem them.

As Jesus weeps outside the tomb of Lazarus he gives validity to the great need for grief work before the resurrection. He invites each participant to proclaim their faith – just as Jesus did to Martha and Mary outside the tomb

– The priest/deacon or minister says:

"I am the resurrection and the Life – He who believes in me will never die – Do you believe this?"

Participants are invited to express their beliefs. Following this, the priest calls them by name and says:

"Come out - In the name of Jesus Son of the Living God, I unbind you and set you free."

Facilitators then help to unravel the burial cloths and bindings.

Touching the Cloak of Christ

We reach out and touch the cloak of Christ after a meditation on the woman with the hemorrhage. Participants are invited to come up to the front of the chapel and touch a cloth that represents the tassel of Jesus' garment. This cloth is draped around the Eucharistic monstrance or a wooden cross in the chapel.

Out loud, they ask him to heal the wounds in their soul which hemorrhage, the bleeding which no one has been able to stop which flows from their broken hearts. These meditations and prayerful exercises are an invitation to express faith – a faith that saves.

The Living Water of Christ

In the ritual, they are invited to come up to a large crystal bowl, the "well of Jacob," husband of Rachel. It is here where Jesus told the Samaritan woman all about her life; that she had lived with many husbands and suffered an abusive history with shame and humiliation. There Jesus promises us Living Water, the opportunity for grace and pointing to the future reality of eternal life. If you drink this water, you shall never be thirsty again. Participants then come to the well and pour water into a glass bowl as they say...

"Lord Jesus, I accept your living water."

All the exercises touch upon fears about new life, obstacles to intimacy with God, and working through deeply repressed memories and feelings of grief.

The Meaning of My Child's Life

Following this ritual, the journey shifts as the participants are invited to develop a spiritual relationship with their aborted children. The activities that follow help them begin to focus on their child's *life*. This is an important stage of grief work because all previous reflection has been focused on the child's *death*. As they search for that meaning, they see that the loss of that child has caused tremendous heartache – sometimes a lifetime of sorrow – and as they begin to reconnect spiritually they discover that their journey has brought them before God. This connection would never have been made in such a real and profound way if it were not for that child's life.

The mothers, fathers, and grandparents receive a personalized letter from the aborted children. This is the one given to the mothers:

> Mother, dear, dear Mother
> could we talk, you and I?
> When I look down from Heaven,
> sometimes I see you cry.
> I want so much to hug you then
> as tight as tight can be,
> Because I think the tears you shed
> are sad, sad tears for me.
>
> Dear Mother, I forgive you,
> O please believe I do!
> It must have been so difficult,
> so very hard for you.
> They told you things would be all right,
> your life would just go on,
> But never said how much you'd weep
> and grieve when I was gone.
>
> Yet we can still be very close
> and love each other, too,
> For though I'm now with God,
> *I'll always be a part of you.*
> So Mother, won't you *name* me, please

and from my Home above,
I'll hear you and I'll come each time
you call to me with love.

I'd like to be the faithful *friend*
 in whom you can confide;
Your *sentinel* before God's Throne,
the *angel* at your side.
So *talk* to me and *sing* to me,
and *pray* with me, please do!
And when you send a smile to me,
I'll send one back to you.

You will notice that two days of work have been done prior
to entering this time of reflection on the child's life. We
have heard of many people who the first time they contacted
a minister or hotline counselor were told to "name their
aborted baby." Without this preparation, the suggestion to
name one's aborted child/children can cause anger, bitterness,
and confusion. When first reaching out for help most people
are too overwhelmed to think in such an intimate way about
their aborted child. The retreat process gently leads them
to the truth with plenty of preparation so that when the
moment comes, they are ready and eager to embrace their
son or daughter.

Naming the Children

This is the appropriate place in the retreat when participants
will name their children. Then they come back up to the
water representing the *Well of Jacob*, which now becomes a
symbol of the baptismal font.

 We read a passage from Lamentations:

"Rise up, shrill in the night, at the beginning of every watch –

pour out your heart like water in the presence of the Lord. Lift up your hands to him for the lives of your little ones."

Following this, the mothers and fathers name their children and say:

"Lord Jesus, I pour out my heart to you and I give you my child"

They light a floating candle and name each child aborted, placing the light into the *Living Water of Christ* that they accepted in the preceding ritual.

Once all the candles honoring lost children have been lit and placed into the bowl, the priest will bless the water as everyone renews their baptismal vows and entrust the children to the mercy of God. This is a beautiful ritual for grieving. The little lights floating on the water represent the souls of the children now with God. Special songs are played as parents join round the bowl and grieve the loss of their children, who have been given names. Special prayers are prayed over the bowl recognizing that they were each created in the image and likeness of God. We pray that their names be enrolled forever in the Book of Life, recognizing their dignity and value as children of God.

This beautiful moment is seared into participants minds – the sensory-based nature of this, and all the *Living Scripture* rituals, enters the mind and soul through music, light, candles, water, meditation, and many other items which are touched, tasted, visualized and emotional energy that can be acted out. The impact on traumatic memory creates an opportunity to reprocess memory. There are powerful brain associations now replacing and redirecting the traumatic memory through a sensory-based process that simply cannot be duplicated through talk therapy or one-on-one counseling alone.

In the next Living Scripture, there is a meditation where participants actually meet their aborted children who they now trust are with the Lord. This is an amazing meditation during which parents and grandparents have a visceral experience of their child. We can't accurately describe the revelation and miracles that occur during this encounter, but it is a tremendous outpouring of amazing grace. Participants have an experience with their child, who loves them and assures them with the hope of reunion one day in heaven.

Bereavement Dolls

Following this meditation, they take a bereavement doll for each child lost. During this therapeutic activity, they are able to release the love and tenderness which has been frozen in traumatic memory. As they release this love and affection they are able to take the action which has been inhibited, locking them into traumatic memory and dissociation. This activity helps to reveal the truth which has been buried in their hearts and rejected from the mind when they surrendered to abortion. The lie was that they did not love or want their child. This activity with the bereavement dolls discharges the blocked energy of love.

Without any directives, participants naturally kiss the babies, cry on them, hold them, rock them, and eventually take them to bed. Those with multiple abortions wrap the symbolic babies in soft buntings and carry them around with a mother's heart. Once the child has become real, they can be mourned in a very deep and authentic way. Being able to physically, emotionally and spiritually express their love and tenderness toward the child is in itself a healing experience.

The group travels together into a new reality, experiencing a glimpse of heaven, and hope for the future. The next stages of the retreat set into motion the "completion" of the trauma – being able to get to the other side of it where it can be transformed into an event with meaning. Only then can the trauma be healed thoroughly, when you can find meaning in what has happened – as one mother embroidered it on her memorial square quilt, *"There is no greater love to give up one's life for one's mom."*

It is never God's will that women and men participate in the death of their unborn children. But in his great mercy, God allows us to find a purpose in all the suffering. The child has actually brought them to encounter God, in a most powerful and intimate way – and they experience the joy and hope of the resurrection within their very flesh. This brings healing and closure, transformation and freedom.

The exercises and meditations continue to proclaim the reality of the child's life in Christ and to help the parents develop a spiritual relationship with their aborted children, embracing them with truth and love. As they reflect on the meaning of their child's life - they discover the truth. They discover the truth of God's love and forgiveness; they discover the truth of the love they denied in their hearts for their own child, they also discover the truth of their child's love, longing, intercession, and forgiveness.

They write letters to their children that will be read at a Memorial Service at the end of the retreat. The letters express love and loss – uniquely written in a way that describes how they envision that child, what they wish they would have been able to enjoy together and express deep sorrow mixed with love. They ask their child for forgiveness, explaining their weaknesses and failings while begging God and the child through intercession to grant them strength and courage in the days to come so they can be reunited in heaven.

On Saturday night there will also be an opportunity for the sacrament of reconciliation for Catholic participants and pastoral guidance and support for Protestant participants. (Rachel's Vineyard is offered in both a Catholic and Interdenominational model.)

Memorial Service and Mass

On Sunday there are some closing exercises and Living Scriptures. There is an opportunity to exchange affirmations and encouragement to the members of the group. The team shares suggestions for aftercare, books, and resources for ongoing healing, a list of counselors, addiction programs, marriage resources, and spiritual directors are provided. Retreatants make commitments to continue growing in faith and wholeness and information about follow-up reunions are distributed.

The retreat culminates with a Memorial Service and a Mass of Entrustment. Family members can be invited to these services and are prepared with some guidelines on confidentiality and what to expect.

During the memorial, the mothers and fathers read the letters they have written. Next, they place their bereavement dolls in a cradle at the altar, light candles, and recite prayers. At the close, they receive a rose and a Certificate of Life that recognizes the child and the parent's deep love for that unique and precious life.

After the closing mass, most retreats conclude with the *"The Banquet of the Prodigal Son."* It's a time to celebrate God's great love and mercy and share fellowship with all gathered.

The Role of Counselor on the Retreat Team

Jessica Slovensky Fouts is a Licensed Professional Counselor, a Certified Clinical Hypnotherapist and a Nationally Certified Counselor with over 18 years' experience in the mental health field.

I asked Jessica to share about her experience serving as a counseling professional in abortion healing ministry:

What was it like when you first starting serving as a counseling professional on a Rachel's Vineyard Retreat team in Atlanta Georgia?

> It was a different experience to move out of the role of directive counselor, to being part of a retreat team. But I soon learned that being a support team member on the retreat was amazing. I was able to see clinically what was going on and to understand the dynamics and subtle nuances of anxiety or fear and non-verbal communication. I was able to be honest and offer comfort without having to analyze it.
>
> It was a time of 'experience', not education, although education certainly occurs during the retreat. I was able to let them "be" at the moment and know that without a doubt, God would pull them through the pain and the anxiety through the Living Scriptures, the retreat process, and through the support and understanding of post-abortive team members.
>
> It has been a tremendous personal, spiritual and professional blessing for me to be involved in the retreats. Being a member of a team approach to helping one heal from abortion is like the

different parts of Christ. We all have certain
gifts that God has bestowed upon us. We use
them for His Glory. It is also nice to realize that
each of us does not have to figure it all out on
our own. We are also able to obtain different
perspectives from various team members."

**How has the retreat helped you in your therapeutic
relationships with individuals suffering after an
abortion?**

The Rachel's Vineyard Retreat responds to the
core issue…not just the presenting symptoms.
I learned the value and power of experiential
meditative work. I saw, immediately, the change
in people once they walked through meditation
and experienced the healing power of Christ.
I have never in my life seen such quick and
effective results with three days of intensive
core work. I feel like I've just been spinning my
wheels with clients for years and that I never
really got to the heart of the issue using just
cognitive work.

Once the retreatant has experienced
such great healing, other areas of her life become
clear. She understands herself and others
better. Issues that were once so confusing
oftentimes become crystal clear so this really
helps in subsequent therapy. Things truly begin
to make sense…her habits and patterns become
understandable and for the first time probably
since her abortion, she is validated and loved
even when the truth is revealed. It becomes truly
an 'ah-ha' moment…actually, it becomes many
'ah-ha' moments! So the group and retreat work

really complements and enhances the counseling experience.

I have found that I am softer as a clinician. My approach was more cognitive-behavioral and not as emotive. This has allowed me to be gentler and kinder and not as heavy-hitting.

CHAPTER TEN

Abortion Recovery Programs: Restoring Marriages and Families

Martha Shuping, M.D., M.A.
President, Ashford Institute
World Congress of Families, Verona, Italy
March 29, 2019 [38]

As a university student in the early 1970's, I was taught that motherhood could be a barrier to women's success in life, and that abortion was necessary for women's happiness and fulfillment. At the time I entered university, abortion was not yet legal through most of the United States, and this teaching was not based on research, but on an unproven theory.

Today, research shows a different picture. In 2005, The Motherhood Study was published, a nationally representative study of more than 2,000 U.S. women, from diverse backgrounds. In this study, 93% of mothers agreed with the statement: "I feel an overwhelming love for my children, unlike anything I feel for anyone else" (Erickson & Aird, 2005, p. 18).

Many mothers were amazed at their overwhelming love for their children, saying that they would be willing to die for their child. A large majority said, "being a mother is the most important thing I do" (p. 20). Only 3% expressed dissatisfaction with being a mother. Women expressed joy in their relationships with their children, despite the reality of responsibilities and sacrifices that were gladly made.

Women begin the process of bonding with their children during early pregnancy. The process is partially mediated by the hormone oxytocin, which can be measured in the woman's bloodstream even in the first trimester, which promotes bonding of mother to child.[39]

Even when abortion is planned, bonding often occurs. In a study of Russian and American women who had past abortions, 37% of Russian and 39% of American women acknowledged feeling emotionally close to the child prior to the abortion.[40] In a study of women at an Australian abortion clinic, 40% acknowledged talking to the fetus, and 30% acknowledged "patting my tummy affectionately".[41] More than half of Swedish women thought of the pregnancy in terms of a child before an abortion and felt a need to do "special acts" after the abortion, such as lighting a candle for the child or apologizing to the child. [42]

A textbook written by abortion providers to teach doctors how to perform abortions has identified that attachment to the child before the abortion is a risk factor for negative emotional reactions after an abortion, and a number of

39 (Feldman, Weller, Zagoory-Sharon, & Levine, 2007).

40 (Rue, Coleman, Rue, and Reardon, 2004).

41 (Allanson & Astbury, 1996)

42 (Stalhandske, Makenzius, Tyden, & Larsson, 2012)

studies have confirmed this.[43]

Many studies have shown that reproductive losses including miscarriage and abortion can often lead to posttraumatic stress disorder (PTSD) in women.[44] In a study of currently pregnant women by Seng and colleagues (2009), 20% had posttraumatic stress disorder, though not related to the current pregnancy. When asked to identify the worst trauma they had ever experienced, the largest number of women said their worst trauma was past abuse, but the second-largest number of women said their worst trauma was a reproductive loss, including miscarriage and abortion.

There are several different types of symptoms that occur in PTSD. One type of symptom is called **"Avoidance."** People who have been through a traumatic experience trying to avoid thinking about it, and to avoid talking about it. They avoid people or places that remind them of the trauma. People avoid this because when they are reminded, it can cause severe psychological distress and sometimes physical symptoms.[45]

When an abortion has occurred, being around babies can be a distressing reminder to women. Rue and colleagues reported that 25% of the American women in their sample had "difficulty being near babies."[46] A woman in Belarus said, "I can't meet with babies. It's too painful. I broke the relationship with my girlfriend who asked me to baby-sit for a few hours with her daughter. I was rude to her."[47] Women have also reported being unable to attend gynecological

43 (Baker & Beresford, 2009; Mufel, Speckhard & Sivuha, 2002; Rue et al., 2004)

44 (Daugirdaite et al., 2015; Seng et al., 2009; Suliman, 2007)

45 (American Psychiatric Association, 2013)

46 (2004, p. SR 11)

47 (Speckhard & Mufel, 2003, p. 8).

exams, also avoiding pregnant women because of distress related to a past abortion.[48]

In a study that compared miscarriage and abortion, women who had past abortions had significantly higher avoidance scores, and the avoidance continued significantly higher after abortion even after five years."[49]

Think for a moment about how persistent avoidance would affect the family. If some women experience distress because their own child is a reminder of the one lost to abortion, this may contribute to bonding problems with subsequent children, and several studies have in fact shown parenting problems and difficulty bonding with children after abortion.[50] Several authors have additionally shown a link between abortion and child abuse and neglect.[51]

Of note, in one study, women who had abortions were compared with women who had no reproductive losses, and also with women who had involuntary losses – miscarriage and stillbirth. Women who had one or more abortions were 114% more likely to have abused their children, while those who experienced miscarriage or stillbirth did not have this increased risk of child abuse.[52]

In addition to problems with the mother-child relationship, avoidance could potentially play a role in marital difficulties. For example, if the husband been involved in the abortion decision, being around him may be a reminder of the

48 (Burke & Reardon, 2002; Speckhard & Mufel, 2003)

49 (Broen, Moum, Bodtker, & Ekeberg, 2005)

50 (Coleman, 2009; Coleman, Reardon & Cougle, 2002; Coleman, Rue & Spence, 2006).

51 (Coleman, Maxey, Rue, & Coyle, 2005; Coleman, Reardon & Cougle, 2002: Coleman, Rue, Coyle, & Maxey, 2007; Ney, Fung & Wickett, 1993)

52 (Coleman et al., 2005)

abortion for the woman. It is also possible for even sexual intimacy to become a distressing reminder of the abortion, if either the husband or wife associates sexual intimacy with having resulted in abortion. In fact, many studies have shown increased sexual dysfunction in both men and women after abortion[53] and also increased separation and divorce.[54]

However, there are many other symptoms of PTSD that can contribute to relationship problems in addition to avoidance. Another category of symptoms involves **negative changes in thoughts and moods.**[55] There are seven types of symptoms within this category; some of these are very clear symptoms that could be harmful to relationships in the family. If the woman is experiencing "feelings of detachment or estrangement from others," or if the woman is "unable to experience positive emotions" such as joy or love[56] one can easily see how this would affect the parent-child relationship or the marital relationship.

Another category of symptoms to consider is called **hyperarousal.**[57] This category of symptoms includes "irritable behavior and angry outbursts...typically expressed as verbal or physical aggression toward people or objects." This category may also include insomnia and reckless/self-destructive behavior.[58] If a woman is chronically sleep-

---

53 (Bagarozzi, 1993, 1994; Bianchi-Demicelli, Perrin, Ludicke, Bianchi, Chatton, Campana, 2002; Bradshaw & Slade, 2003; Coleman, Rue & Spence, 2006; Coyle et al., 2010; Fok, Siu, & Lau, 2006; Miller, 1992; Rue et al., 2004; Speckhard & Mufel, 2003; Tornboen, Ingelhammar, Lilja, Moller & Svanberg, 1994)

54 (Barnett, Freudenberg, Wille, 1992; Bracken & Kasi, 1975; Coleman, Rue & Spence, 2006; Freeman et al., 1980; Lauzon, Roger-Achim, Achim, & Boyer, 2000; Rue et al., 2004).

55 (American Psychiatric Association, 2013).

56 (American Psychiatric Association, 2013, p. 145)

57 (American Psychiatric Association, 2013)

58 (p. 145)

deprived and frequently angry, one can see that this is likely to have an adverse effect on parenting and on the marital relationship; if the anger is addressed physically, this may be a factor related to the research showing increased child abuse after abortion.

To be clear, not every person who is exposed to a potential trauma develops PTSD. Not every woman who has an abortion develops PTSD, but some do, and other women may have some of the symptoms without meeting all the criteria for a diagnosis of PTSD. Men also can develop PTSD after abortion. Because of the large numbers of abortions that take place worldwide, many marriages and many families are suffering from the effects of abortion.

However, there is some very good news that you can use in your country, and that is: research shows that spiritually based abortion recovery programs are helping women and men to heal from the effects of abortion. Research has been done using psychological tests before and after the Rachel's Vineyard weekend retreat, at nine sites in the U.S. and Canada, showing that avoidance and hyperarousal symptoms were reduced to a statistically significant degree, and that shame also decreased while self-esteem increased.[59] In the same study, before and after testing was done for the SaveOne program, a once a week support group for abortion recovery. Although the number of participants was low these results also showed similar statistically significant results.

These two programs, SaveOne and Rachel's Vineyard are particularly noteworthy for several reasons. Both of these programs are available in numerous languages and many countries around the world- Rachel's Vineyard in more than 70 countries on six continents, and SaveOne in more than 50 international locations. In addition, both of these programs allow husband and wife to attend together so that

59 (Jaramillo, 2017).

they can process their grief and distress together which seems to promote healthy marriages, though there is no research directly on the effects on the marriage – yet those who conduct these retreats have seen the results of couples resolving abortion-related issues and being able to enjoy their relationship again.

Those who conduct Rachel's Vineyard retreats also have heard women say how this changes their relationship with their children – they may become able to enjoy their relationship with their living children for the first time.

To be clear – there is data showing significant decreases in shame, avoidance, and hyperarousal in individual women, but there is no research to date on the effects on the family. However, when you consider the symptoms of PTSD and the likely effect of those symptoms on relationships within the marriage and family – one can see that reducing these symptoms could help the family.

A 2004 study by Susan Layer, also showed similar benefits from two other support group programs, *Forgiven and Set Free*, and *Surrendering the Secret*.

All the programs included in this research are spiritually based programs, rooted in the Christian Scriptures, though people of any faith are welcome to attend, and occasionally Buddhist, Muslim, and Jewish women have attended, as well as atheists, who are welcome to participate to the extent they choose, though most participants are Christian.

In my book, *The Four Steps to Healing* (Shuping & McDaniel, 2007), I explain that many women feel a need to address four specific issues or relationships after an abortion: their relationship with God, their grief related to loss of the child, their relationships with others involved in the abortion decision, and their own self-esteem which often suffers in the abortion experience. These issues are addressed within the context of Christian spirituality in the four programs studied.

Martha Shuping, M.D.
Psychiatrist
President, Ashford Institute

REFERENCES:

Allanson, S. & Astbury, J. (1996). The abortion decision: fantasy process. *Journal of Psychosomatic Obstetrics & Gynaecology* 17, 158-167.

American Psychiatric Association (2013). *Desk Reference to the diagnostic criteria from DSM-5.* Washington, D.C.: Author.

Bagarozzi, D. (1993). Posttraumatic stress disorders in women following abortion: Some considerations and implications for marital/couple therapy. *International Journal of Family and Marriage,* 1, 51–68.

Bagarozzi, D. (1994). Identification, assessment and treatment of women suffering from post-traumatic stress after abortion. *Journal of Family Psychotherapy,* 5(3), 25–54. doi:10.1300/j085V05N03_02

Baker, A, & Beresford, T. (2009). Chapter 5, Informed consent, patient education and counseling. In M. Paul, E. S. Lichtenberg, L. Borgatta, L., D. A. Grimes, D.A.P. G. Stubblefield, & M. D. Creinin, M.D. (Eds.). *Management of Unintended and Abnormal Pregnancy: Comprehensive Abortion Care.* Chichester, UK: Wiley-Blackwell.

Barnett, W., Freudenberg, N., & Wille, R. (1992). Partnership after induced abortion: a prospective controlled study. *Archives of Sexual Behavior,* 2, 443-455.

Bianchi-Demicelli, F., Perrin, E., Ludicke, F., Bianchi, P.G., Chatton, D., & Campana, A. (2002). Termination of pregnancy and women's sexuality. *Gynecologic and Obstetric Investigation,* 53, 48-53. *BMJ Open* 6, e009698 doi:10.1136/bmjopen-2015-009698

Bracken, M.B., & Kasi, S. (1975). First and repeat abortions: a study of decision-making and delay. *Journal of Biosocial Science*, 7, 473-491.

Bradshaw, Z., & Slade, P. (2003). The effects of induced abortion on emotional experiences and relationships: A critical review of the literature. *Clinical Psychology Review*, 23, 929-958.

Broen, A. N., Moum, T., Bodtker, A. S., & Ekeberg, O. (2005). The course of mental health after miscarriage and induced abortion: a longitudinal, five-year follow-up study. *BMC Medicine* 3(18).

Burke, T., & Reardon, D.C. (2002). *Forbidden grief: The unspoken pain of abortion*. Springfield: Acorn Books.

Coleman, P. K. (2009). The psychological pain of perinatal loss and subsequent parenting risks: Could induced abortion be more problematic than other forms of loss? *Current Women's Health Reviews*, 5, 88-89.

Coleman, P. K., Maxey, C. D., Rue, V. M., & Coyle, C. T. (2005). Associations between voluntary and involuntary forms of perinatal loss and child maltreatment among low-income mothers. *Acta Paediatrica, 94*, 1476 – 1483.

Coleman, P.K., Rue, V.M., & Spence (2006). Intrapersonal processes and post-abortion relationship challenges: A Review and consolidation of relevant literature. *The Internet Journal of Mental Health* 4,(2). Retrieved from http://ispub.com/IJMH/4/2/3804

Coleman, P. K,, Reardon, D.C., & Cougle J. (2002). The quality of the caregiving environment and child developmental outcomes associated with maternal history of abortion using the NLSY data. *Journal of Child Psychology and Psychiatry and Allied Disciplines, 43*, 743-758.

Coleman, P. K., Rue, V. M., Coyle, C. T., & Maxey, C. D. (2007) Induced abortion and child-directed aggression among mothers of maltreated children. *The Internet Journal of Pediatrics and Neonatology, 6.*

Coyle, C.T., Coleman, P.K., Rue, V.M. (2010). Inadequate preabortion counseling and decision conflict as predictors of subsequent relationship difficulties and psychological stress in men and women. *Traumatology,* XX(X), 1-15. doi: 10.1177/1534765609347550

Daugirdaite, V., van den Akker, O., & Purewal, S. (2015). Posttraumatic stress and posttraumatic stress disorder after termination of pregnancy and reproductive loss: A systematic review. *Journal of Pregnancy, 2015*(646345). doi: 10.1155/2015/646345.

Erickson, M.E., & Aird, E.G. (2005). The motherhood study: Fresh Insights on mothers' attitudes and concerns. New York: Institute for American Values. Retrieved from http://americanvalues.org/catalog/pdfs/the_motherhood_study.pdf

Feldman, R., Weller, A., Zagoory-Sharon, O., & Levine, A. (2007). Evidence for a neuroendocrinological foundation of human affiliation: Plasma oxytocin levels across pregnancy and the postpartum period predict mother-infant bonding. *Psychological Science,* 18, 965-970.

Fok, W.Y., Siu, S.S.N., & Lau, TK. (2006). Sexual dysfunction after a first trimester induced abortion in a Chinese population. *European Journal of Obstetrics & Gynecology,* 126, 255-258.

Freeman, E.W., Rickels, K., & Huggins, G.R. (1980). Emotional distress patterns among women having first or repeat abortions. *Obstetrics and Gynecology,* 55(5), 630–636.

Jaramillo, S. (2017). Mending broken lives: Post-abortion healing. (Doctoral Dissertation). Retrieved from ProQuest Dissertations and Theses (Accession Order No. 10274360). Retrieved from http://gateway.proquest.com/openurl?url_ver=Z39.88-2004&res_dat=xri:pqdiss&rft_val_fmt=info:ofi/fmt:kev:mtx:dissertation&rft_dat=xri:pqdiss:10274360 839-846.

Lauzon, P., Roger-Achim, D., Achim, A., & Boyer, R. (2000). Emotional distress among couples involved in first trimester abortions. *Canadian Family Physician,* 46, 2033-2040.

Layer, S.D., Roberts, C., Wild, K. & Walters, J. (2004). Post-abortion grief: evaluating the possible efficacy of a spiritual group intervention. *Research on Social Work Practice,* 14(5), 344-350.

Miller, W.B. (1992). An empirical study of the psychological antecedents and consequences of induced abortion. *Journal of Social Issues, 48,* 67-93.

Mufel, N., Speckhard, A., & Sivuha, S. (2002). Predictors of posttraumatic stress disorder following abortion in a former Soviet Union country. *Journal of Prenatal & Perinatal Psychology & Health, 17,* 41-61.

Ney, P. G., Fung, T., & Wickett, A.R (1993). Relations between induced abortion and child abuse and neglect: Four studies. *Pre and Perinatal Psychology Journal 8,* 43-63.

Rue, V.M., Coleman, P.K., Rue, J.J. & Reardon, D.C. (2004). Induced abortion and traumatic stress: a preliminary comparison of American and Russian women. *Medical Science Monitor, 10*(10), SR5-16.

Seng, J.S., Low, L.K., Sperlich, M., Ronis, D.L. and Liberzon, I. (2009). Prevalence, trauma history, and risk for posttraumatic stress disorder among nulliparous women in maternity care. *Obstetrics and Gynecology, 114*(4).

Shuping, M. (2016). Abortion recovery counseling. In R. MacNair (Ed.), *Peace psychology perspectives on abortion* (pp. 115-136). Kansas City, MO: Feminism and Nonviolence Studies Association.

Shuping, M.W., & McDaniel, D. (2004, 2007). *The Four Steps to Healing,* (Non-denominational Edition). Tabor Garden Press: High Point. (ISBN-10: 0972876944).

Speckhard, A., & Mufel, N. (2003). Universal responses to abortion? Attachment, trauma, and grief responses in women following abortion. *Journal of Prenatal & Perinatal Psychology & Health, 18*(1), 3-37.

Suliman, S., Ericksen, T., Labuschgne, T., de Wit R., Stein, D., Seedat, S. (2007). Comparison of pain, cortisol levels, and psychological distress in women undergoing surgical termination of pregnancy under local anaesthesia versus intravenous sedation. *BMC Psychiatry, 7*(24). doi:10.1186/1471-244X-7-24

Stalhandske, M.L., Makenzius, M., Tyden, T., & Larsson, M. (2012) Existential experiences and needs related to induced abortion in a group of Swedish women: A quantitative investigation. *Journal of Psychosomatic Obstetrics & Gynaecology 33*(2), 53-61. doi: 10.3109/0167482X.2012.677877

Tornboen, M., Ingelhammar, E., Lilja, H., Moller, A., Svanberg, B. Evaluation of stated motives for legal abortion. *Journal of Psychosomatic Obstetrics and Gynecology, 15*, 27-33.

CHAPTER ELEVEN

An Invitation to Healing

By Lori Eckstine

I had an abortion at age sixteen which negatively altered my life in many ways. Those painful effects lasted until 2000 when I went on a Rachel's Vineyard retreat in Texas at age forty-six. My retreat experience profoundly changed and renewed my life which led me to help bring the Rachel's Vineyard retreats to my home state of Oregon in 2001. For eleven years I also served as the Project Rachel Coordinator for Catholic Charities of my Diocese, developing teams and leading retreats in the Portland and Bend areas.

I helped start a nonprofit corporation called "Project Aurora" so we could expand the retreats in the mid to southern Oregon area." I developed and led the teams for Project Aurora in Eugene and Southern Oregon. Since 2001 I have led 52 retreats and seen nearly five hundred women and men receive healing from the destructive lies of abortion.

Given the prevalence of abortion in our communities, it is likely that we will encounter people in our daily life or in our ministry relationships affected by abortion. Our words and actions can penetrate the walls of protection, denial, anger,

and avoidance - or cause them to withdraw further behind
their self-protective fortress of fear and anxiety.

The Initial Contact - Building on a Solid Foundation

I began my pro-life ministry journey volunteering for a
pregnancy support center. This experience was extremely
important as I learned the essential skills of peer counseling.
Of great assistance was the book *Introduction to Pregnancy
Counseling* by Sister Paula Vandegaer, LCSW.[60] The chapter
entitled "Post Abortion Counseling in a Short Term Setting"
was especially helpful in building a basic foundation for
ministry communications in an effective and compassionate
language. Each chapter ends with review questions that help
the reader personally process and integrate the material.

Learning to normalize a client's feelings and behaviors, or
lack of normal feelings is a critical part of an initial phone or
email encounter with a post-abortive individual. Sr. Paula
stresses the importance of creating an encounter where a
woman or man is given permission to have feelings about
abortion. Drawing upon Sr. Paula's work, let's look at how to
effectively address the abortion loss. This will be especially
helpful in a setting where the abortion may not be the
presenting problem, but the individual has disclosed this in
their history:

> – Given the sensitivity of the issue, it can be helpful to
> address the abortion in a context of other pregnancy
> losses -- miscarriage, abortion, or the tragic loss of a
> baby.

> – Be brief and simple, but accepting and understanding.
> The client's response will indicate which direction the
> conversation will go and if she wants help:

60 Vandegaer, V. (1999). *Introduction to Pregnancy Counseling.* International Life
Services.

– Ask: *"Do you ever feel kind of down about the whole incident?"* A lot of women and men need to talk with someone after their abortion because they have private feelings and concerns.

– Share:

> "Sometimes unresolved issues of grief from miscarriage or abortion can cause a lot of confusing and painful thoughts, emotions, and behaviors. These losses are very real and most people benefit from seeking help to sort through their feelings. Would you like to learn more about ministries that are very effective in helping those impacted by abortion find healing and peace? They will listen to you and answer your questions. Here's the contact information."

– For those that deny any problems following the abortion you can share:

> "I'm glad you're okay now. Some women and men feel depressed, think about their baby, have trouble sleeping because of nightmares, have regrets, or other problems in their lives. If you ever have any of those things happen to you or have feelings you're struggling with, please feel free to contact me."

It is critical in our initial contacts with those hurting after abortion, that all our actions and words reflect the love and mercy of God and the sure hope of reconciliation and healing. Each encounter and step in the healing process prepares the person for the next phase in the recovery experience. The most important step in that journey is often that initial confession, email or counseling contact.

If you reflect on the love and mercy of God and prepare with some simple guidelines, you can be a partner with the Holy

Spirit to guide the wounded soul to the Light of Christ. With practice, you can become skilled in the basic principles to speak with sensitivity and effectiveness about the issue of abortion. Remember that nothing is ever forced and we must respect that people have their own time and season to begin the healing process. Everything we do is a gentle invitation.

Here are some other important issues to consider in the early stages of the ministry relationship:

– Commend them on their courage. Acknowledge and affirm the fact that they have made the difficult and very important decision to seek healing. Give them your full attention and be mindful of what they ask and how they ask it. Don't let your mind wander or rush ahead from feeling pressure or anxiety. You don't have to make it happen…but be fully present to the individual, trusting the Lord and the process.

– Michelle Krystofik, former Associate Director of Respect Life for the Archdiocese of Newark shares about the gift of listening:

"The most important this is to listen. This has been a secret, deeply painful wound that they may be sharing for the first time. So it is essential to do a lot of listening initially and then to affirm that their feelings are common to those who have experienced abortion."

– Use their first name a couple of times in the conversation

– The conversation will progress if you can maintain a calm disposition and if your understanding mannerisms are combined with statements that carefully send affirming messages. Paradoxically, those affirming messages can effectively touch on abortion symptoms.

They can be introduced by *"Perhaps, you have felt.... or "Sometimes others have felt..." or "I felt."*

– If they came to you through a website like Rachel's Vineyard or another referral source, ask them what motivated them enough to make this contact with you.

– Encouragements with hope-filled statements are powerful. Many individuals have suffered for years and can be skeptical that there really is help for them. Use additional words expressing mercy and compassion.

– Reassure them it is normal when they have opened up to someone about their abortion that painful memories may come forth or they may have strong feelings later such as anxiety or fears – that this is normal. Invite them to call if this happens so you can talk it through. Let them know they can call or email you (or the team counselor) anytime.

– Here are some possible closing statements to use as your conversation comes to an end:

> "Julie/John, there is hope and there is healing. I've seen many broken hearts and broken lives just like you, find healing and peace at our Rachel's Vineyard retreats. There will volunteers serving on the retreat team who have experienced abortion and understand how you feel. I hope the material I'm sending you will demonstrate that...I can send you the information so you can look it over and have time to think about it more. I hope to hear back from you... please look at our website and feel free to call or email again if you want to."

Sometimes you may encounter a caller who feels desperate and is asking about your abortion recovery program as a final effort to find relief from her pain. A contact person must be comfortable in hearing the painful symptoms after abortion loss, and any traumatic or painful events and circumstances of their lives. Often those experiences have led to much suffering. This further suggests the importance of reading a book like *Forbidden Grief* as part of the preparation for post-abortion ministry. With attentiveness, your contact/ correspondences will provide awareness and insights into that person's relationships, ways of coping, patterns of behavior, and may give clues to possible childhood traumas.

It may point to their natural gifts, significant life experiences, and virtues – all of which she probably has been unable to see. You can begin to acquaint them with the beautiful and courageous person she is. Your compassionate qualities will help the wounded person to face the truth and embrace the cross that stands before her/him with the sure hope of resurrection. In addition to your retreat or support group information, you can provide referrals for counseling support, emergency suicide hotline number if necessary, and spiritual direction.

Helpful Post Abortion Ministry Resources

It is essential to educate yourself about post-abortion grief and trauma. I recommend the following:

> The exceptional and comprehensive book *Forbidden Grief: The Unspoken Pain of Abortion* is a good place to start.

> Visit *Rachel's Vineyard (Rachelsvineyard.org)* and *Silent No More Awareness Campaign (SilentNoMore.com)* websites to read and view the testimonies of men and women who have experienced abortion loss. It is important to understand the necessary components of the healing process and the importance of effective ministry resources.

An excellent series called **Detaching with Love**, by Fr. Emmerich Vogt, is an audio series with tools to help separate one's personal issues and needs from ministry service. (**Detaching With Love**. The 12-Step Review. 2001 NW 94th Ave., Vancouver, WA 98665 www.12-step-review.org)

The USCCB has a brochure entitled, *How to Talk to A Friend who's had an Abortion*. Respect Life Program 866 582 0943. There is a teen version, item #0120 or an adult version, #0016. Spanish, Item #0121. An additional handy guide from the USCCB is entitled *TIPS*.

Dr. David Reardon's *How to Help Others Find Healing, and Do's and Dont's* can be found at www.afterabortion.org

Introduction to Pregnancy Counseling, Sister Paula Vandegaer, L.C.S.W. International Life Services 1999.

Kevin Burke, LSW • Theresa Burke, Ph.D • Rev. Frank Pavone

CHAPTER TWELVE

Pastoral and Sacramental Concerns

By Father Frank Pavone

Pastoral Observations on Confession and Counseling

Abortion has many victims beyond the child who is destroyed. Were all the abortions to stop tomorrow, the Church's work of healing these other victims will have only begun. Since abortion was legalized, the number of ministries dedicated to healing people from the wounds of abortion, as well as the number of those seeking such healing, has only increased.

The moment of confession

When a penitent confesses the sin of abortion, the priest or minister must walk a balance between two possible traps. First of all, he must inspire the women or man with hope and make it clear that God and the Church forgive this sin. The priest at this moment brings one of the most critical elements to the process of healing after abortion. He affirms for this woman or man that God still loves and accepts him or her, without in any way minimizing the evil that has occurred. At the same time, it is important not to make the penitent feel that everything can or should go back to the way it was before. It can't change anymore than it can for a parent who has lost a child of age 5 or 20. A child has died, and they are changed forever. There will always be pain and grief there that is legitimate. Our counsel at this moment is to both assure them of forgiveness and to assure them that it is quite normal to continue to suffer from the abortion. Feelings of horror regarding what has happened do not mean she is not forgiven. But they do mean that there is a wound that needs attention and healing.

Fr. Pat Scanlan, who serves on the Rachel's Vineyard Team in Cork Ireland, shares his insights on the Sacrament of Reconciliation:

Since my involvement with Rachel's Vineyard, I have a much deeper sense of compassion for the penitent who struggles to put into words the fact that they have had an abortion. Sometimes it is a word they can barely utter. I have come to realize that they don't want me as a priest to indulge in false compassion and make little of their sin. That would be to deny the reality of their experience of guilt and grief and become a collaborator with those who would have them continue to live in denial. Every fiber of their being knows that what happened was terribly wrong. They need to meet Jesus who will speak the truth with love. The priest's words, attitude, and body language need to convey love, tenderness, and understanding while upholding the truth of the Church's teaching on abortion. We have no better model than Jesus and how he treated the woman taken in adultery: "Neither do I condemn you. Go now and sin no more." Normally I will have a few Rachel's Vineyard leaflets in the Confessional, and I will pass one to the penitent and encourage them to participate in a weekend. Some of these have contacted me later to say how much the experience of Confession and the R.V. weekend changed their lives.

Repeat Confessions

Women and men can go to confession many times and still not *feel* forgiven. Sometimes they will go to multiple priests, confessing the same sin over and over again, feeling tortured by their inability to fully accept the grace that the sacrament offers.

This is closely connected to the complicated grief that frequently accompanies the experience of abortion.

Let the penitent know that while some people find a resolution of their abortion-related pain and remorse through the experience of confession, it is common for individuals to still suffer from feelings of shame, guilt, and difficulty with self-forgiveness even after confession. Some women and men will continue to confess the sin over and over again because they interpret their continued painful symptoms and/or behaviors after abortion as a sign that the sacrament "didn't take," or God did not forgive them.

You can let them know that reconciliation may be an important foundation of a healing process but that an important next step for many people is a program of emotional and spiritual healing. If appropriate, have some contact cards or pamphlets with you that you can share with the penitent. Consider placing this information permanently on the Church bulletin.

Penance for Abortion

Penance for abortion has to both be substantial and have a definite closure. Some priests, for example, ask penitents to offer a week of special prayers, perhaps the Rosary or special periods of adoration, Scripture reading, or other forms of prayer. In such cases, penitents should be reminded that if they forget the practice on a given day, this does not affect the forgiveness of the sin. Other priests advise that the penitents have Masses offered for the child, by going to a parish (carefully not indicating that it should be the parish in which the confession is being made) and requesting Masses for a special intention.

Many women and men repenting of abortion may feel inclined to become active in the pro-life movement, especially to help others avoid the mistake that they made. Such a step can be extremely helpful for them and for the movement. Such individuals deserve careful guidance in this area to assess what form of pro-life work they should engage in. Before speaking about their involvement in abortion, they need to have arrived at a certain level of peace and healing and need to be sure that they have told the people close to her about it before they speak publicly. The Silent No More Awareness Campaign (www.SilentNoMore.com), of which I serve as Pastoral Director, provides helpful guidance and discernment in this area and is one of the avenues through which those who are called to share their testimony can do so.

What happened to my baby?

This question will also be part of the healing process, and we answer it by strengthening the person's hope and trust in the goodness and mercy of God. The goal here is more the strengthening of one's trust and confidence than the crafting of precise conceptual answers. Doctrinally, we know the necessity of baptism, and we also know that God gives all the opportunity to be saved. While the Church has not pronounced on the question of how these truths interact in the case of aborted children, she certainly urges us to hope and trust. This is especially true in the words of St. John Paul II in Evangelium Vitae 99, where he directly addresses those who have had an abortion:

> "I would now like to say a special word to women who have had an abortion. The Church is aware of the many

factors which may have influenced your decision, and she does not doubt that in many cases it was a painful and even shattering decision. The wound in your heart may not yet have healed. Certainly what happened was and remains terribly wrong. But do not give in to discouragement and do not lose hope. Try rather understanding what happened and face it honestly. If you have not already done so, give yourselves over with humility and trust to repentance. The Father of mercies is ready to give you his forgiveness and his peace in the Sacrament of Reconciliation. To the same Father and to his mercy you can with sure hope entrust your child. With the friendly and expert help and advice of other people, and as a result of your own painful experience, you can be among the most eloquent defenders of everyone's right to life. Through your commitment to life, whether by accepting the birth of other children or by welcoming and caring for those most in need of someone to be close to them, you will become promoters of a new way of looking at human life."

Clergy in the Vineyard

The loving welcome and understanding of a representative of God and the church can be that essential first step on the journey of healing. This encounter may be in the confessional, counseling or in spiritual direction. Fr. Rafael Garcia S.J. shares some valuable insights from his ministry serving in El Paso Texas:

Fr. Garcia, please share with our readers your impressions from that initial encounter with someone who needed healing after abortion.

The wounds of abortion are deep. There is much "stored" pain, guilt and shame. The woman is very fragile, emotionally, as she begins to share the pain-event. It's a hurtful secret that has often been kept for many years. It takes trust in the other(s) for the woman or man to share the story of the abortion.

An attentive and compassionate presence and listening are crucial. One should not be quick to provide answers or even interrupt the conversation, falsely thinking that quickly moving through the painful subject or trying to diminish the importance of the event will be helpful.

Touch on your role as a spiritual director, confessor, and counselor as a priest working with such individuals.

One needs to be compassionate, present, truly listening, and usually, to not say much. We need to in a sense, "get out of the way" -- so God can act in the encounter. Be conscious to not transmit any body language or verbal language that could be interpreted as judgmental or that one is in a hurry. It's important to point out in the conversation, that God is merciful and forgives -- anything -- since often the feeling of the woman is that this was an unforgivable sin. One must also mention that forgiveness of self is crucial. I think that awareness of one's own brokenness, sin, failures, and pain is extremely important in understanding the other person's brokenness, failure, pain, etc.

What challenges have you faced in your ministry relationships as you help people heal after an abortion? What would be helpful to share with your fellow clergy?

It's a challenge to deal with other issues and moral dilemmas in the woman's lives that are still unresolved. This challenge is not uncommon in pastoral care in general. It is important to encourage "follow-up" care and ministry to continue the healing and support process after a Rachel's Vineyard retreat.

In pastoral care, if a woman or man shares that they had an abortion, and it is obvious that they are still hurting, encourage them in the short time that may be available, and provide a ministry name and phone number, so as to connect them with a good healing resource.

Please share your experience serving on a Rachel's Vineyard Team.

The process and format of the Rachel's Vineyard retreat are certainly one that is Spirit inspired. I'm always amazed at how two or three hours into the retreat the first night, the participants are sharing very personal and painful aspects of their life. I'm always moved to share something of my own wounds in the retreat and other team members do the same. In the short format of fewer than 48 hours, a great sense of trust and knowing each other is achieved and this is wonderful. This level of intimacy in sharing is something that is not easily achieved in groups and I think not even in families.

Celebrating the various rituals that the priest does in the retreat is very consoling and humbling. Celebrating the Sacrament of Penance and the Eucharist are also graced moments. The very presence and participation of a priest throughout the whole retreat is something positive that the woman or man probably has not experienced, namely, that a priest could be "accessible" and not distant "up in the altar" or "behind the curtain" in the confessional. *This is important* **given the understanding of Catholics that the ordained priest is** *a "representative" of God, and so the* **closeness and accessibility** *of the priest is a reflection of the closeness and accessibility of God.*

It's a joy to compare how the woman looked on Friday when she came to the retreat anxious and fearful and then Sunday at the final Mass of the retreat, the faces of the participants show happiness; peace and her clothing and make-up are

125

bright, etc. It's an outward sign that something wonderful has happened "inside"... I think that the format of the Rachel's Vineyard retreat is Spirit-inspired, an effective instrument for God to heal.

Fr. Pat Scanlan P.P., has been serving in Parish ministry since his ordination in 1977 for the Diocese of Cloyne, Ireland and has been a member of the Rachel's Vineyard Retreat team in Cork since 2003:

Fr. Pat, how long have you been involved in ministry to those wounded by abortion?

Since my ordination to the priesthood in June 1977, I have met with many women and some men who have been wounded by abortion. Almost invariably they were crying out for forgiveness and healing. In my experience, the celebration of the Sacrament of Reconciliation marks a decisive step in their journey towards recovery. Yet I have always felt that they needed something more. What that something was, I was not so sure. Yes, the sin had been forgiven, but they had a deep need for healing and restoration.

How did you get involved with Rachel's Vineyard?

In the summer of 2003, I had a phone call from a good friend Bernadette Goulding who shared with me her excitement at having discovered a movement called Rachel's Vineyard. Everything she said convinced me that this was the answer I had longed for over many years. I agreed immediately to become involved.

The first Rachel's Vineyard weekend in Ireland was held in Cork in October 2003. We were very fortunate in that from the outset we had the blessing and support of my bishop, Most Rev. John Magee. I was not on the team for that weekend, but I have participated in about fifteen weekends since that time.

Can you share from your experience serving as a member of the Retreat Team?

Being involved in these weekends certainly ranks among the most rewarding experiences of my priesthood. The essential role of the priest on a Rachel's Vineyard Retreat is to be present as one who really listens. By simply being present to them as they journey through their pain and grief towards hope and healing the priest is making present the gentle compassionate Christ who cares deeply for his wounded sisters and brothers.

It is not an exaggeration to say that on each weekend we experience miracles of grace. The participants usually arrive bowed down by too many years of grief and self –loathing. Slowly, gradually as they enter into the process of the weekend they get in touch with, express, release and reconcile deep painful emotions.

The Sacrament of Reconciliation, which is made available to those who want it on Saturday night, is a beautiful experience for both penitent and priest. Both begin to realize the truth of the statement "The church is a hospital for sinners and not a hotel for saints." As they leave to return home on Sunday afternoon, many of them will have experienced the Mercy of the Lord at a very deep level. A grace that is truly amazing has touched wounded hearts and made them beloved disciples who will in-turn become instruments of his compassion to others. Some, because of their newfound freedom, will in due course speak out and become part of a grassroots movement that will one day replace the present Culture of Death with a Culture of Life. I feel I am one of the most privileged of priests to have had this experience so many times and I encourage all priests, deacons, and seminarians to "come and see" at least once.

Kevin Burke, LSW • Theresa Burke, Ph.D • Rev. Frank Pavone

How has your work in healing those wounded by abortion impacted your preaching?

Prior to my involvement in Rachel's Vineyard, I often felt a bit scared at the prospect of preaching the Gospel Of Life. I was conscious that in any congregation there may be one or more who had experienced abortion, and I was never sure how to effectively proclaim the truth while at the same time witnessing compassion. The truth without compassion is a lethal weapon, particularly for wounded souls. Compassion without the truth is a cruel deception. Now I actually enjoy preaching the Gospel of Life. I know from my experience of Rachel's Vineyard that the Gospel is truly Good News for these women and men, who have fallen victim to one of the great lies of our time. I usually tell my congregation that what I want to share is what I have learned from women and men, who have had abortions and how the Good Shepherd is waiting to embrace, heal and forgive them. I share in a gentle compassionate way that abortion wounds the lives of mothers and fathers. I know that if there are women present who have had an abortion they will identify, and realize that the church wants to help them. I have had people come to me afterward to find out more about Rachel's Vineyard. For the remainder of the congregation, when I then proceed to present the church's teaching on the right to life of the unborn it is but an obvious and positive conclusion to be embraced, once they have heard a little about the wounds that follow abortion.

Fr. Peter O'Brien is a parish priest in the Archdiocese of Portland and one of the many priests who serve on the regional Rachel's Vineyard retreat teams. Fr. Peter beautifully captures the heart of post-abortion healing:

> *Rachel's Vineyard is a special place, a journey into human wounded-ness, weakness and corruption…to the very depths of our sin. The journey leads into the pain, but it does not end there. The retreat is an utterly holy place*

128

*where God's infinite love is encountered burning away our
impurities and restoring life and beauty to the soul. When
a person leaves the retreat, Rachel's Vineyard remains a
place of the heart and soul. The process of healing has
begun.*

Loving Them Both:
How to Preach About Abortion
By Fr. Frank Pavone

"Father, I came into this Church this morning being
totally pro-abortion, and the homily changed my views
completely."

"Father, I had an abortion, and sometimes it hurts
to hear about it, but please keep up the preaching! I
gladly endure whatever pain I have, because I know the
homilies will keep some other woman from ever going
through what I have gone through from the abortion
itself."

"Hi! I'd like to begin this letter by thanking you for
last week's homily. I was deeply moved and so was my
younger brother. I'm 17 and he's 12. We did not fully
understand what goes on in abortion until your homily.
We both would like to get on the mailing lists of pro-life
organizations."

These are three of the thousands of reactions I have received
after preaching about abortion over the years. The reactions
cited above are characteristic of the content and tone of the
others as well.

How do we preach on abortion? What are we trying to

accomplish? How do we awaken our people to this immense evil? How do we handle reactions of anger and disagreement?

Where are our people on abortion?

A good place to start answering these questions is to examine the attitudes of the American people on abortion. Sometimes we hear that "Most Americans are pro-choice." The statement is meaningless until the term "pro-choice" is defined. A more helpful way to understand what most people think is to ask them the specific circumstances in which they think abortion should be legal.

That is precisely what various surveys have done over the years (see www.PriestsForLife.org/statistics). Questions vary, but a common model asks people if they think abortion should be a) always prohibited; b) permitted only to save the mother's life; c) permitted only for rape, incest, and to save the mother's life; d) permitted only in the first three months of pregnancy; e) permitted throughout the first six months of pregnancy, or f) permitted at any time during pregnancy, and for any reason.

Consistently, the majority of Americans hold one of the first three positions, not the second three.

By the admission of the Alan Guttmacher Institute, the abortions in cases of rape or incest account for about 1 percent of the total abortions. By the testimony of numerous medical experts, furthermore, abortion (*the killing of the child*, as distinct from early delivery) is *never* necessary to save a mother's life.

Conclusion? Most Americans oppose 99 percent of the abortions taking place, while the current policy on abortion (available through all nine months) is supported by a small minority of the public.

We likewise see the curious phenomenon that among the

majority of Americans who would oppose most abortions but permit some, there is a growing number of those who are willing to admit that the abortions they would consider justified are the killing of human beings. In a CBS/NY Times poll, some 50 percent of the respondents were willing to call abortion "murder," yet one-third of those people said it is sometimes the best course of action for the woman to take.

What is going on here? Why are there so many abortions when most people oppose them and even admit what they are?

The Conflicted Middle

First of all, people have gotten the message from the pro-life movement that abortion takes the life of an unborn child. They have also gotten the message from the abortion-rights side that sometimes abortion benefits women, who should not be deprived of the benefit. Having accepted both messages, the majority of Americans belong to the "conflicted middle." Where this group ultimately goes is where America will ultimately go on abortion.

An important dynamic at work in this group is denial fueled by pain. There are more people each day who are directly involved in an abortion decision and are therefore at least initially not eager to get involved in an effort to either expose what it is or to stop it.

There is an even larger number, however, whose pain over abortion is not because of direct personal involvement, but because of a dilemma that was best described by one who said, "When people know enough to realize that to learn a little more will involve some risk, it is amazing to see how little they want to learn." People know abortion is happening, but also realize that if they look at it too directly, they will not be able to live at peace with themselves unless they start to do something to stop it. At the same time, they know that if they try to stop it, there will be a price to pay. They may lose friends or face other kinds of opposition. They don't want to make the sacrifice necessary to confront injustice.

What, then, is their solution to this dilemma? Ignore the problem altogether. Denial protects them from the pain of the situation. This is why some people become angry when the topic of abortion is raised. They were succeeding in ignoring it, and someone brought it to the surface.

What Do We Need to Convince People of?

Given the attitudes people have on abortion, and the dominant images they have about the pro-life effort, we can begin to trace several themes we need to communicate as we preach on this topic.

People need to know that we are on their side. A discussion of abortion, whether in private or public, should acknowledge the pain that most of us feel about it, whether we describe ourselves as pro-life or not. The psychological attitude to take and to convey is, "You are not my enemy. We are in this painful situation together and need to help each other out of it." The individual who may react angrily to a pro-life homily is best approached with a frame of mind similar to which we care for those afflicted by personal disasters. We are dealing with good people who have pain, not with enemies.

People need to know that *to be pro-life is to be pro-woman*. The difference between "pro-life" and "pro-choice" is not that pro-lifers love the baby and pro-choicers love the woman. The difference is that the "pro-choice" message says you can separate the two and the pro-life message says you cannot. Pro-lifers are criticized for being "fetus-lovers" who are insensitive to women. *But one cannot love the child without loving the mother.*

Abortion defenders claim they are loving women, even as they admit they are killing their children. *But one cannot love the woman without loving the child. Nor can one harm the child without harming the mother.*

The message must be clear that to be pro-life means to be pro-woman, and that the challenge the pro-life movement gives to society is, *"Why can't we love them both?"*

Equal Rights for Mother and Baby

One reason why many who think abortion is wrong will not actively oppose it is that they think they have to make a choice between defending the rights of the baby or those of the mother, or that they have to consider the baby as more important than the mother:

The authentic pro-life message is a message of equality. It is a challenge to expand the circle of our love, welcome, and protection.

This insight helps resolve the conflict of the "conflicted middle," who see the evil of abortion but think it benefits women. People need to know that to oppose abortion does not mean to oppose those who have them. An aspect of the pro-woman theme of our pro-life preaching is the healing and forgiveness the Church and the pro-life movement offer to those who have been involved in abortion. In most of my homilies, I mention that one woman I encountered had undergone 25 abortions, and proclaim that even for her, the doors of the Church are open!

The Church has the perfect spiritual and psychological balance necessary for those who have been involved in an abortion. The last thing such a person needs to hear is, "What you did is no big deal." The nature of the grief after abortion is that the individual involved in the abortion has begun to realize precisely what a big deal it was! Now, this person needs someone to tell her that she should not feel silly for feeling sad, that there is indeed a reason for the grief in her heart, and that what her heart is telling her is true: she and the father participated in the death of their unborn child. A great disservice was done both to her and her child when someone convinced her that the abortion would be "no big deal." Accepting that line was a major act of denial. Healing now begins when she breaks out of denial and calls the evil what it is. The clear preaching of the Church about abortion helps her to do this.

At the same time, the other line she does not need to hear is, "You are rejected; there is no hope." As a woman or man realizes the evil that has occurred, they will be tempted to sentence themselves as guilty of the unforgivable crime. The Church, however, contradicts that despair with the clear message of forgiveness echoed recently by the Holy Father in *Evangelium Vitae* #99. The Church accompanies all who have been involved in abortion, whether the mother, father, grandparents, siblings, other relatives, friends, clergy, or even the abortionists and their staff, to the forgiveness and healing Christ offers.

Those in the pain of abortion are not helped by silence. Some refrain from preaching about abortion out of the sincere motive of not hurting women who have had abortions. Yet that silence does not interpret itself. The person grieving over abortion can infer from our silence that we do not know her pain, or that we do not care, or that there is no hope. None of this is true. By our clear and compassionate homilies, we can break through the silence, which led her to this disastrous choice in the first place.

De-Isolate The Issue

People need to know that abortion *is their business*. The key challenge in presenting our people with the abortion issue is not so much convincing them that it is wrong, but rather convincing them that it is any of their business. Abortion defenders will say, "If you are against abortion, fine…don't have one, but leave the rest of us alone to exercise our own beliefs and make our own choices." Many people who oppose abortion will therefore lament it, but will feel out of place trying to stop it. They see it as wrong, but as a private wrong, with which it is none of their business to interfere.

One of the key tasks necessary here is to de-isolate the issue. People understand that we have to intervene to help the poor, victims of abuse, the drug addict, the victim of crime and war. Even if we do not know their names, or have never seen the faces of these victims, we know it is our business to help them. We do not hear people say, "I would never abuse my child, but if the other person wants to do so, that's her choice." The reason people do not say that is that they realize that some choices have victims. When somebody's choice destroys or threatens somebody else's life, that's everyone's business. It is, after all, the business of love, which intervenes to save our brothers and sisters in need. There, precisely, is the reason it is both our business and our privilege to work to stop abortions.

People need to know that there is something they can do to stop abortion. All of the above is not yet enough. Many oppose abortion but do not think anything can be done. If we awaken people to the evil but do not guide their response, they will either end up depressed or perhaps act irresponsibly. The problem is not that there is nothing that can be done, but that there are not enough people doing the perfectly legal, peaceful and effective activities they can do to end abortion. Presenting such options in the homily, and following up on them through well-organized parish respect life programs, will overcome another obstacle to the involvement of many in this cause: they think of the pro-life movement as an extreme and fanatical movement characterized by activities they want nothing to do with.

How do we convey all this in 10 or 15 minutes? -- Three Elements for a Pro-Life Homily

A very convincing homily can be given in ten minutes conveying the points mentioned above and incorporating the strategic elements I have explained. Priests for Life offers specific homily training and resources at www. ProLifePreaching.com, and through my book, *Proclaiming the Message of Life* (see ProclaimingTheMessageOfLife.com).

The basic homily structure I have used around the nation consists, in conjunction with the readings, of three major points in the following order.

1. **There are alternatives to abortion.** Those who have abortions do not do so because of "freedom of choice," but rather because they feel they have no freedom and no choice. Many are "pro-choice" not because they like abortion but because they ask, "How can the woman live without it?" The good news is that the Church and the pro-life movement are providing better choices than abortion and that a wide range of help is available for anyone who needs it. Thousands of helping centers provide financial assistance, medical services, legal advice, counseling, a place to live, jobs, education, and assistance to parent the child or make an adoption plan. People at Mass can be asked to take a handout that has phone numbers and websites of abortion-alternatives which they can pass on to those who might need them (such as the Option Line at 1-800-712-HELP, PregnancyCenters.org). It is amazing to see how many people who know that the Church opposes abortion are unaware of the Church's willingness

to provide alternatives. This makes them feel good about being a Catholic and about helping the pro-life movement. By mentioning the point about alternatives first, a major objection is tackled before it arises: "What are you who oppose abortion going to do to help the woman who needs it?"

2. **Stress that the Church offers forgiveness and healing after abortion.** This is critical because so many feel they cannot be forgiven. If all the abortions ended tomorrow, the mission of healing will have only begun. The Gospel of Life is a Gospel of Mercy. The hope of mercy, furthermore, prevents additional abortions, since there are significant psychological dynamics whereby despair leads to repeat abortions. (About half of abortions in America are repeat abortions.) Furthermore, many hesitate to become active in the pro-life movement because they think that to oppose abortion means to oppose those who have had them, and they do not want to compromise their relationship with their sister, cousin, or friend. If they see that being pro-life means embracing these women and men with forgiveness, they may be more inclined to join the effort.

3. **Help people to see through the slogans that make tolerance of abortion seem so reasonable.** The term "Pro-choice," for example, fails to point to what is chosen, and would never be applied to child abuse or violent crime. Some choices have victims, including the choice of abortion. "Safe and legal abortion" is a slogan that misleads people into thinking that if it is legal, it must be safe, and to keep it safe we need to keep it legal. Yet the abortion industry is the most unregulated surgical industry in the nation, and

regularly destroys the health and lives of the women who procure it in legal facilities. Also, focus on some basic facts that most people are unaware: nothing takes more lives than abortion, with thousands happening daily in America; it is legal and happens through all nine months of pregnancy; rape or incest accounts for about 1% of them.

The practical follow-up to the homily is a handout I mention when I talk about alternatives. It is a Priests for Life brochure entitled "You Can Save Someone's Life Today!" It contains dozens of practical things people can do to help stop abortions, including toll-free numbers (like 1-800-712-HELP) that can be dialed from anywhere in the nation and have a live person at the other end 24 hours a day to provide counseling and any type of assistance for those who are tempted to have abortions or who have had them. This handout is placed at all the exits of the Church, and everyone is asked to take it home, read it, keep it, and use it. I have received letters explaining that the handout was used successfully to persuade a person not to have an abortion, and to lead others to heal after abortion. You can contact us at:

Priests For Life
Web: www.Priestsforlife.org
Email: mail@priestsforlife.org
Phone: 321-500-1000

The Church has all the tools necessary to heal our land. Let us go forward, then, in this ministry of reconciliation, with a spirit of courage, peace, and joy!

Reaching Out With the Love of Christ

How can clergy reach out with the good news of healing in
a sensitive and effective way? Here are some helpful ideas to
assist you in your ministry:

– Our response must always be a gentle invitation to
healing offered within a message of love, hope, and
encouragement.

– The Lord through His Church extends His love, mercy,
and forgiveness to all who have participated in abortion
and seek reconciliation and forgiveness. Reassure those
suffering that post-abortion healing in the archdiocese
is offered by professionals and laypersons many who
experienced their own abortion healing and understand
the pain and fear of opening up this wound.

– Because abortion often leads to a complicated type of
grief, different from normal experiences of loss, a special
healing process is often helpful in bringing peace and
healing to those that suffer. This is best accomplished in
the context of a healing retreat, support group, or bible
study where the individual progresses through steps of
healing, which will involve naming their unborn child,
asking forgiveness, expressing grief and love, with the
sure hope of reunion in the life to come.

– We suggest sharing with your congregation the role
that unhealed abortion grief can play in individual and
relational difficulties. *(Sample homilies in Appendix II to
assist you.)* Assure your parishioners that with healing,
they will discover the deep peace and relief of symptoms
associated with abortion loss. Share with them the
good news that through this healing God will bless
and strengthen their marriage and family relationships

making them stronger than ever.

– Have a woman or man working with your local ministry of healing after abortion share their experience of abortion loss and healing in a talk after communion. *(Sample witness talks also found in Appendix III.)*

– Share Paragraph 99 from *Evangelium Vitae* on the message of mercy and encouragement from John Paul II.

– Lori Eckstine with Project Rachel in the Archdiocese of Portland suggests Priests include information about the symptoms following abortion, and the opportunities for healing, as part of the normal curriculum in RCIA, in returning Catholic groups such as Landings, in youth groups, Cursillo, TOTB series, in Engaged Encounter, Marriage Encounter, and Retrouvaille›s take-home packets, at retreat centers, parish run soup kitchens, etc. *A growing number of ministry participants trace the onset of their healing path to one of these sources.*

– Local memorial stones to the unborn provide validation to the grief of those who have lost children to abortion. Such stones can be given a special place on Church property. Individuals may also commemorate their aborted children by having a plaque in their honor placed in the National Memorial for the Unborn (6230 Vance Rd, Chattanooga, Tennessee 37421, phone 800-505-5565). Flyers are available from the Memorial›s office.

In the National Memorial for the Unborn is a painting of a mother with her child in her arms. It is called *I Will Hold You in Heaven* and expresses the hope we offer to every mother, father, and other relatives who have lost a child to abortion. It is necessary to face the reality that the child died. In coming to terms with that reality, we also embrace the fuller reality that death has been conquered. The one who should have been held on earth, and whose absence now causes such pain, will indeed be held one day when death shall be no more and every tear will be wiped away.

May every priest and deacon, and spiritual leaders in all Christian denominations, as a minister of the Gospel of Life, effectively extend this hope to the world.

Kevin Burke, LSW • Theresa Burke, Ph.D • Rev. Frank Pavone

CHAPTER THIRTEEN

Marriage Preparation: Preventative Care for Couples with Abortion History

A Rachel's Vineyard Retreat Facilitator from the Midwest shares about a couple that attended their Rachel's Vineyard Retreat:

> "The girl had an abortion before she met her fiancée. On their engaged encounter weekend, she felt a strong desire to share this with him. The priest gently invited them to consider attending our Rachel's Vineyard retreat before they got married the following month, and they immediately signed up. It was so beautiful to see how supportive this young man was of her throughout the weekend. But it was also touching to hear some of his own story. They will have such a beautiful and holy marriage because it is rooted in the love and spirituality that they now share together."

Given the number of couples impacted by abortion, (or will be tempted to abortion when facing an unplanned or complicated pregnancy in their engagement period, or after marriage) it makes good sense to find ways to reach out with the good news of healing in marriage preparation programs.

Encourage those involved with marriage preparation in your

faith community to consider the possibility of including abortion healing information and resources in their information packets. This can be done with sensitivity and respect for confidentiality if this is made part of the overall program that all participants learn about.

Remember that in working with individuals that have experienced trauma, everything we offer is a gentle and hope-filled invitation. *Nothing is ever forced.* If we educate couples and make healing resources available to them, we can help them avoid some of the common relational problems that can ultimately end in divorce.

Here is a message you can share with couples in marriage preparation and place in their packets of information:

Be Not Afraid: An Invitation to Healing

Abortion is a sensitive and painful issue for those that have experienced the procedure. It is also a difficult subject for those who may have encouraged or assisted another person to have an abortion. The Church reaches out with love and understanding to you today.

You may be feeling anxious right now just to hear or read about this topic. This is understandable. Try to relax and open your heart to this message, because it is one of hope and healing offered with compassion and concern.

Most individuals struggle with two opposing reactions to their abortion. Usually, they want to put the event behind them as quickly as possible and move on with their lives. However, there is an equally powerful need, often unconsciously expressed, to make sense out of the experience, find an outlet for their painful and confusing feelings, and discover reconciliation, healing, and peace.

This hidden grief can emerge in some of the following symptoms:

Private addictions and compulsions - Fear of Pregnancy - Parenting difficulties – Challenges with intimacy and communication - Anger issues - Extramarital affairs arising out of unhealed grief and shame - Anxiety and depression.

This buried pain that may not surface until the onset of a wanted pregnancy, or may occur when another stressful life event or relational crisis occurs. Not everyone who has a history of abortion will experience these symptoms. However, you may experience more hidden and private grief that can take away from the fullness of joy, intimacy, and love that God wants you to experience in marriage.

There are effective healing programs that will empower you to embrace the challenges and joys of married life with joy and confidence, building a strong, healthy and faith-filled marriage.

It is natural that you may be fearful to open this area from your past. But rest assured the volunteers, counselors and clergy/ministers involved in this ministry understand your pain and loss and will respect your confidentiality. Many of them have experienced abortion and know how scary it can be to take the first step or even think about sharing this secret.

But those that have made the rewarding journey to healing would tell you that it is well worth the effort, and will bring great blessings to your marriage and family life. You will find a brochure in your packets with information on how to find a confidential abortion healing program.

[This could be a time to have a couple from a local abortion healing program share about their healing journey.]

A Couple Heals A Marriage Is Saved

The following article is courtesy of the **Fairfield County Catholic –Diocese of Bridgeport Connecticut**

BRIDGEPORT, CT – An abortion ravages three people: the child, the mother, and the father. While post-abortion counseling has usually focused on the mother, a Rachel's Vineyard retreat sponsored by the Diocese of Bridgeport offers fathers, too, a chance to experience healing and forgiveness. The next retreat will be held September 19-21. One married couple that attended a Rachel's Vineyard retreat together this year spoke recently with *Fairfield County Catholic*. For confidentiality purposes, in this article, they are called Mary and Joe.

Fairfield County Catholic: Why don't you begin by explaining the circumstances that drove you to an abortion?

Mary: Joe and I were both in college, and had been dating a couple of years. The first time we had intercourse, I got pregnant. I came from a large family and my parents, who were devout Catholics, made a lot of sacrifices for my education. I was too ashamed to tell them I was pregnant. There was no one to reach out to.

Couldn't you reach out to your boyfriend?

Mary: I told Joe I was pregnant, and that I would have to get an abortion. I was waiting desperately for him to say something, to tell me we'd manage somehow. It never happened.

Joe: I knew it was wrong, but I was silent. I never stood up for the baby. I prejudged her and decided that her mind was made up. I was angry with her for choosing an abortion.

Most couples break up after an abortion because the guilt

and pain are so great. Yet you stayed together and got married. You were clearly very much in love. How did the aftermath of the abortion affect your marriage?

Mary: We still loved each other, and we were committed to our marriage. My feeling of anger at Joe was pushed down for so many years that I didn't even recognize it. But it was there all the time. I took my anger out on him without ever recognizing where it came from.

Joe: There was a lack of trust in our relationship. I blamed her for the loss of the baby. I did things that purposely hurt her. I drank a lot, I gambled, I did a lot of things to escape into a private world where I wouldn't feel pain.

You are both practicing Catholics, raising your children in the faith. Didn't you talk to a priest about what happened?

Mary: After years of this, it became apparent that it was something I had to deal with. I had confessed my abortion to three priests over the years. After the fourth priest, I began to accept that God could forgive me.

Joe: There were years and years of anger and heartache and being distant from God. I did talk to a parish priest, a good man, about the abortion. But I couldn't go to God about it. I think men are so proud, they don't see what they've buried. It was all kept inside and it was destroying me. I deliberately did things to keep my own self-esteem down. I considered suicide. At one point, I remember walking downstairs with a gun and a suitcase; Mary stopped me.

What happened when you went into the Rachel's Vineyard retreat?

Mary: It felt confidential, safe, and welcome. There was an overwhelming sense of peace knowing that so many people were praying for us. Everybody there, although each story was different, the pain was similar. With them, we were able to let our guard down.

Joe: I didn't want to go to Rachel's Vineyard to begin with. I walked in there on a Friday evening thinking, "I'm going to re-live all this stuff I've been avoiding for so long." I think men are reluctant to go to these things openly and be part of it.

Why was this retreat so effective, when you had both already been to Confession and received absolution years ago?

Mary: My big breakthrough came when I was able to express my anger at Joe. He had never realized that the abortion had any connection to our behavior. We were able to forgive each other and to have our baby forgive us.

Joe: I sat there and literally cried during some of the sessions. I was able to express my anger toward myself at my total lack of courage. Once I released that, it's easier to accept and take ownership of the acts that I did. I came out completely exhausted, mentally and physically. It's given me the confidence to be a person again. I still feel awful about what happened, I still feel ashamed, and still feel the guilt. But there are no deep-rooted vindictive acts occurring. I'm able to stop and think where I would instinctively go the wrong way before. I feel reborn. I've been accepted by God, my wife, and, most of all, by myself.

What would you say to married couples that have gone through an abortion, either before or during their marriage?

Mary: Rachel's Vineyard gives you the tools to expose hurt feelings. It puts you back in contact, and you can go on from there. There's no need to suffer anymore.

Joe: For married couples that are dealing with the aftermath of an abortion, if the man doesn't come on retreat with his wife, he won't understand what she's been going through. He just won't get that. And he will still carry around the shame and the guilt. It's a tremendous loss of opportunity for him.

Where do you go from here?

Mary: We're still in counseling. Rachel's Vineyard isn't a magic fix. It gives you the tools to heal, the tools to get back in contact. We can get angry when we talk about finances, or try to work out what to do with some problem with the kids. But it's not this deep, dark anger that comes from nowhere.

Joe: I'd like us to be as close as we can possibly get. I'd like to re-kindle a courtship, to walk hand-in-hand, spend more time together – and more time together in prayer.

Kevin Burke, LSW • Theresa Burke, Ph.D • Rev. Frank Pavone

CHAPTER FOURTEEN

Abortion Recovery Ministry with Sexual Abuse Survivors

Women who have experienced sexual abuse and abortion trauma can present some challenging relational dynamics for clergy and counselors. A better understanding of these issues is important for safe and effective ministry.

– A survey by the Elliot Institute reported that 21 percent of women who had abortions reported a history of childhood physical abuse and 24 percent reported childhood sexual abuse.[61]

– Another study indicates nearly one-third of American women are physically or sexually abused by a husband or boyfriend at some point in their lives.[62]

With the growth and success of Rachel's Vineyard, founder Theresa Burke was asked to provide training and education for clergy/ministers, counselors and laity in Catholic dioceses across the U.S. The following case study is a fictional account based on themes found in a variety of troubling pastoral relationships between clergy and women with abortion and

61 Burke, T. (2002). *Forbidden Grief: The Unspoken Pain of Abortion*. Acorn Press.

62 Schoen, C. (May 1999). *The Commonwealth Fund, Health Concerns Across a Woman's Lifespan: 1998 Survey of Women's Health*. The Commonwealth Fund. CommonWealthFund.org

151

sexual abuse histories.

This reflects the more challenging situations one may encounter in ministry and is not necessarily reflective of the majority of the population served. But given the potential pain and suffering for all involved, it is important to learn from those pastoral relationships that became toxic over time.

Case Study

> Fr. Tom greeted Susan as she arrived for the first appointment for spiritual counseling. Susan was referred to Fr. Tom by the abortion healing outreach of her diocese.
>
> Fr. Tom was eager to share the love of Christ and to be a good listener. As their ministry relationship developed, Father learned that Susan suffered from multiple abortions and also had been sexually abused by an uncle between the ages of 8-12. Acting out of the shame and boundary violations of her childhood, Susan became promiscuous in her adolescence. She endured her first abortion at the age of 16.
>
> Like many victims of trauma, she would go on to repeat the themes of her unhealed wounds. Susan experienced two more abortions before marrying her current husband and eventually gave birth to two children. Susan never shared her previous abortions with her husband and kept this a closely guarded secret. Underneath the cheery and attractive exterior was a deeply wounded soul struggling with anxiety, self-loathing and difficulties in her marriage.
>
> Fr. Tom looked forward to their meetings together. Susan confided that she never encountered the love, compassion, and mercy of Jesus Christ as deeply as what

she felt through their relationship. He humbly gave glory to God while enjoying their deepening ministry connection.

Fr. Tom began leading Susan through the steps of abortion healing. It was after their 4th meeting that he noticed a change in the relationship. Susan began to call him more frequently in between their scheduled appointments. Sometimes, she would stop by the rectory without notice. More disturbing, as Fr. Tom gently began to address this issue, Susan became very distraught and angry. In a fit of rage and tears, she blamed him for not caring about her feelings and needs.

Being a kind-hearted man, he naturally felt distressed by these accusations and offered to see her for an additional appointment that week. He wanted to reassure her and help ease some of her anguish. Fr. Tom appreciated their ministry relationship and was hopeful that with some improved communication and trust, they could continue working together through her healing process.

Unfortunately, the intensity of Susan's emotional attachment continued to escalate. Fr. Tom gradually became irritated by her expectations, especially given his other responsibilities in the parish. He was beginning to feel trapped in a relationship that seemed to be spiraling out of control. Fr. Tom tried to re-establish relational boundaries and limit his contact with her.

Consequently, he began to emotionally distance himself; phone calls from Susan went unanswered and he did not have the energy to respond to the many e-mails she continued to send. His withdrawal only served to increase her feelings of abandonment and rejection. This dynamic multiplied her frantic attempts to make contact with him. Vacillating between desperation and anger,

Susan struggled with powerful feelings of dependency and betrayal coupled with the desire to show him how much suffering his actions were causing.

Beneath the rage, Susan reasoned that because Fr. Tom did not want to be near her, neither did God. This reinforced a core wound in her personality that had existed since childhood; she was defective, dirty, unwanted and unlovable. Furthermore, Susan interpreted this rejection by a representative of God as further proof that she was unredeemable. Even God did not want to be closer to her.

One-on-One Ministry with the Sexually Abused Woman

It is important to be aware of some additional dynamics that can complicate ministry relationships.

- Some women with histories of sexual abuse and abortion may have a tendency to sexualize their relationships with men. This is a pattern deeply rooted in their relational histories. They have been conditioned to respond to men who give kindness, warmth, and support – they feel obliged to give back, frequently confusing kindness and care with sexual attraction.

- After all, the individual has learned in her previous relationships with men that she is only of value when she is sexual. Therefore, this pattern is transferred to the new ministry relationship. The relationship can become flirtatious and sexualized, which means that strong feelings of attachment and sexual desire are coupled with a yearning to satisfy or possess the giver in return.

- There can be a tremendous drive to recreate traumatic themes from abuse and abortion within the context of the pastoral relationship. A common example is the desire to engage in secrets and forbidden taboos. A fantasy or an actual affair with a clergyman or counselor can be part of the re-creation of these traumatic themes.

Joanne explains:

> "Being intimate with a priest or deacon (who represents the holy and undefiled) even in fantasy, made me feel closer to God. I soon developed an unhealthy emotional and spiritual enmeshment with the priests I went to for spiritual direction and counseling. I now understand after my healing retreat that I was trying to redeem something unholy and impure deep inside my heart and soul.

> But prior to healing, I would re-create in these relationships conflicts laden with guilt and shame from my childhood and from the abortions as I became "the temptress" who wants to defile the holy. It's a very painful and confusing experience because you really are trying to get closer to God and find healing and also hunger for a deeper emotional and spiritual connection with others.

> It was just too intense and triggering to try and do that whole abortion healing process with a priest or in spiritual direction. Since my retreat, I have much healthier relationships with priests and deacons, especially those that have served on the retreats in our area. They really understand the pain of abortion and how to safely accompany us in our healing journey with spiritual guidance and sacramental ministry."

Preying on the Vulnerable

A clergyman or lay minister with the following

characteristics are at great risk to enter into an abusive and exploitive relationship with a woman with abortion and sexual abuse history:

> Has poor boundaries and a history of exploitation in their relationships; lacks deep humility and self-awareness, and tends toward arrogant and/or narcissistic behavior; is emotionally/sexually immature; has unmet emotional needs that arise from areas of unresolved grief and loss; suffered past emotional/sexual/physical abuse and has not had intensive emotional and spiritual healing.

Clergy, pastoral staff, and Counselors must understand clearly the need for professional and ministry boundaries. They must be aware of unmet emotional needs and personal areas that need ongoing conversion. They must be transparent and regularly accountable in ministry or counseling relationships with another counseling professional or clergyman. Even with such boundaries in place, a woman can experience powerful and confusing emotions that lead to an unhealthy dependence on a singular caregiver.

This helps us to see the wisdom of expanding the circle of support early in the ministry relationship with deeply wounded women and making the appropriate referrals for abortion healing groups and counseling. A healing network helps lower the intensity and dependence in the relationship in its early stages and enables the minister to offer the love of Christ, the grace of the sacraments, and spiritual direction that are so essential in the healing journey.

Women and men are blessed by the sacramental ministry and spiritual guidance of pastors and deacons. Ministers in all faith communities can face similar difficult issues in their peer and pastoral relationships. If you make appropriate use of retreats and support groups, counselors, and lay ministry assistance you can proceed with confidence knowing you are part of a healing team.

Kevin Burke, LSW • Theresa Burke, Ph.D • Rev. Frank Pavone

CHAPTER FIFTEEN

Let That Light Shine!
Ten Ways to Promote Your
Abortion Healing Ministry

By Susan Swander and Kevin Burke, LSW

Keep in mind that people often need to hear messages about abortion loss and recovery a number of times before they are ready to take that next step, and reach out for help. It can be years before that seed you planted bears fruit.

Here are 10 ways to promote your abortion recovery ministry:

1. Meet with your Pastor/Minister
Contact the pastor or another minister active in your church. This kind of personal connection is important. You or someone on your team can share about a past abortion, faith-related struggles after the procedure, and how healing of your abortion loss was such a blessing.

Most pastors are not sure how to address the issue of abortion. Some fear hurting or alienating those that had abortions. Your personal sharing will be a valuable education about the issues women and men struggle with after the procedure. It can also open the door to a ministry partnership as you assist the pastor in reaching out to those in the congregation hurting after abortion.

2. Notices in Church Bulletins

Susan shares: 16 years ago in October 2003 my life was changed forever. I went to Mass at my local parish church and picked up a bulletin as I left. When I arrived home, I perused the bulletin with my cup of coffee. And, then I saw IT.

IT was a small box ad in the bulletin saying something like this:

> "Suffering after an abortion? There are hope and healing available at a Rachel's Vineyard Retreat. More confidential information is available at www. Rachelsvineyard.org or by calling this local number."

That was the first time I had ever heard of Rachel's Vineyard ministry. As I read through their website, I wept buckets of tears. It was the first time in 36 years that I had acknowledged my suffering after abortion. That website offered me hope. It took me a few days to make that phone call listed in the box ad. But I finally did – I knew it was time.

Several months later I attended a Rachel's Vineyard retreat. What a remarkable healing experience this weekend was. Words do not do justice to the love, compassion, and understanding I found during the retreat. Later I went through a mentoring process and became part of the team offering the retreats in Oregon. Rachel's Vineyard gave me my life back.

Thank God for that tiny little box ad in the church bulletin. What power it held for me.

3. Testimony During Church Services

Susan: "After healing and with careful discernment, I felt called to share my abortion story. I have shared my testimony of pain and hope at a number of churches throughout

Oregon. I have been moved by how many fellow church-goers also suffer after abortion, or know someone who does."

4. Create an uncluttered, engaging, easy to navigate website so people can learn about your ministry. Donors are often interested in helping out with such a project and a tech-savvy person from your church community could assist with set up.

5. Connect with the local Christian radio stations in your area – and some national shows as well. Let the program director know that you have women and men who can share about abortion loss and recovery. This is especially helpful around the time of the March for Life, Mother's Day and Father's Day and for Catholic Christians in the month of October (Respect Life Month) when media are more open to our message.

6. Social Media Cultivate a current team member, volunteer, or alum from your abortion recovery ministry to help develop a social media presence on Facebook, Twitter, and Instagram. Once you get the hang of it this is an effective way to create brief messages and images to promote recovery resources and share about your ministry.

7. Tear-off flyers on church bulletin boards, pamphlets and drop cards that provide info on your website, social media, and contact number. It's important to have such contact resources with you when you share your testimony or to share with friends, family or anyone who may benefit from healing.

8. Contact your local churches, seminaries, and Catholic/ Christian educational institutions. Let them know you are available to share with their students and ministers-in-training about abortion loss, the ways this can impact women and men, and the road to recovery. This is a great way to help them better understand and reach out to their future congregations.

9. Connect with the campus ministry and pro-life groups at secular colleges in your area and offer to share your testimony with the students, how to best reach out to abortion-minded students based on your experience, and resources for recovery for those that had abortions.

10. Prayer, Support, and Networking - Come together regularly as a team and pray for God's Spirit to give you wisdom, discernment, and patience. Consider registering with the *Silent No More Awareness Campaign* (www. SilentNoMore.com) and find women and men in your area who are called to speak out about abortion loss and recovery. This is a great way to find support and network with others in your area and nationally that share a heart for this outreach.

CHAPTER SIXTEEN

Sermons on Abortion and Abortion Healing

SERMON I:

Liberty and Freedom for Captives

*[Deacon Tom Rasmussen was ordained as a Permanent
Deacon for the Diocese of Charlotte by Bishop Donoghue.
In 1997, Deacon Tom earned a Master of Arts Degree in
Counseling, and he was a Licensed Professional Counselor.
Deacon Tom ministered on Rachel's Vineyard Retreats in the
Diocese of Charlotte, North Carolina. Deacon Tom has passed
on to the Lord, and we are so grateful for his many years of
service in the Lord's Vineyard, sharing the love of Christ and
His Church to those wounded by abortion.]*

Jesus was sent to proclaim liberty to the captives and to set
the oppressed free.

About ten miles west of Charlotte, North Carolina is the
beautiful Belmont Abbey, a Benedictine Monastery and a
Catholic Liberal Arts College. The campus church is the
Basilica of Mary, Help of Christians. If you were to visit the
Basilica you'd find an unusual Baptismal Font.

It is a large rock, about five feet or so across and somewhere
around three feet high. The stone's surface is relatively flat. A
place on that flat surface has now been hollowed out to form

a basin for the waters of Baptism.

In a shameful period of our history, that rock was the platform for black slaves to stand on so they could be seen as they were auctioned to the highest bidder. There is a real paradox in that Baptismal Font. Through the waters and grace of Baptism, that rock, which once brought people into captivity, into slavery, now brings people into freedom as God's children.

The inverse can also be true: freedom can bring people into slavery. January 22 is the anniversary of the Supreme Court's decision in the case of Roe v. Wade. That decision said abortion was a freedom guaranteed by the Constitution of the United States.

Sadly, that freedom brings about slavery. Untold millions of people who sought freedom from an unwanted pregnancy have become enslaved by the consequences of their actions. For so many, the aftermath of abortion has become a nightmare, filled with shame and humiliation, with guilt and despair, filled with remorse and depression. Each individual's story is unique, but their varied stories are united by feelings of unworthiness, hopelessness, helplessness, and self-condemnation. For so many, the memory of the abortion is vividly clear and painful even years later.

While the word choice has become synonymous with abortion, for most it is not really a choice at all. Studies show that 70 percent of the women choosing abortion believe it is morally wrong and 54 percent were unsure of their decision even as they made it. These facts show women are choosing abortion not because they think it is the right thing to do, but because they think, due to whatever circumstances they are facing, it is the only thing they can do. Not seeing any alternatives, they feel trapped.

Many women are openly threatened by loved ones that if they keep the child they will lose the love and support they need from their boyfriend, husband, or even their parents. One young girl was begging the abortionist to stop and let her keep her baby, but her mother had driven her to the clinic, her mother had paid the money and signed the consent, and her mother insisted the abortionist do what he had been paid to do.

Husbands give their wives the ultimatum, "You can have the baby or you can have me, but you can't have both of us." One woman went to her fiancé with the joyful news they were to be parents. He handed her some money and said, "Here's my share. You got us into this mess; you get us out of it."

Others feel that their future career plans will be destroyed by an unplanned pregnancy. For example, some young women are convinced they cannot keep their baby and finish college. Still, others fear losing the chance to have the type of home or the type of lifestyle they always planned. Some feel they cannot care for the baby.

Whatever form the pressure takes; it is the evil one who is whispering, "Sure babies are good. But not now! You're not ready for it. It will ruin everything. Nothing will ever be the same again. You have to save what you have. An abortion will give you back control over your life. Then you can save what you have, save the love of the people for whom you and this baby will be just another burden. You can save your career. You can save your future. Make this little sacrifice now, give up this pregnancy and wait for another day, and you won't have to lose anything." That's Satan's great lie...

There is hope. Saint Pope John Paul II wrote *Evangelium Vitae*, The Gospel of Life. Listen closely to his words in that encyclical

I would now like to say a special word to women who have had an abortion. The Church is aware of the many factors which may have influenced your decision, and she does not doubt that in many cases it was a painful and even shattering decision. The wound in your heart may not yet have healed. Certainly what happened was and remains terribly wrong. But do not give in to discouragement and do not lose hope. Try rather understanding what happened and face it honestly. If you have not already done so, give yourselves over with humility and trust to repentance. The Father of mercies is ready to give you his forgiveness and his peace in the Sacrament of Reconciliation. You will come to understand that nothing is definitively lost and you will also be able to ask forgiveness from your child, who is now living in the Lord. With the friendly and expert help and advice of other people, and as a result of your own painful experience, you can be among the most eloquent defenders of everyone's right to life. Through your commitment to life, whether by accepting the birth of other children or by welcoming and caring for those most in need of someone to be close to them, you will become promoters of a new way of looking at human life.

As the Pope wrote, the first step is admitting what happened and receiving God's Peace and Forgiveness in the Sacrament of Reconciliation. But many have confessed their abortion repeated times and received the Lord's forgiveness, yet they can't forgive themselves. They still need spiritual and psychological healing. Very few counselors are sensitive to the deep psychological, spiritual and relational damage abortion causes.

Rachel's Vineyard is an international healing ministry of Priests for Life. A Rachel's Vineyard weekend retreat is a safe place to renew, rebuild and redeem hearts broken by abortion. Weekend retreats offer a supportive, confidential and non-judgmental environment where women and men can express, release and reconcile painful post-abortive emotions to begin the process of healing. The retreat can help a person experience God's love and compassion on a profound level. It creates a place where men and women can share, often for the first time, their deepest feelings about their abortion.

Our late Pope told mothers who had abortions, "You will also be able to ask forgiveness from your child, who is now living in the Lord." A Rachel's Vineyard Retreat provides an environment of emotional and spiritual safety in which a parent can ask forgiveness from their child, and can grieve for the child.

Outcome studies have proven the effectiveness of the Rachel's Vineyard Retreats. I have been part of the presenting team on three retreats, and I am awed at the healing that takes place. If anyone wants to learn more about Rachel's Vineyard, you can find it on the website www. rachelsvineyard.org. The website and the telephone numbers for retreats in our diocese are in this week's bulletin.

Psychological, relational, and spiritual healing can, in turn, lead persons to become, as Pope John Paul said, "the most eloquent defenders of everyone's right to life." Some time ago, the diocesan newspaper ran an article about a woman at one of the Charlotte abortion clinics, standing quietly off by herself, holding an "I regret my Abortion" sign. I'm not certain of the exact number, but I think the paper said twenty-three women in one month alone got back in the car and drove off after talking to her.

Jesus said let the one who is without sin cast the first stone. It is unfortunate that some have become so preoccupied with the horrible reality of abortion that they assume those who have abortions are horrible people. This is neither true nor fair. Sin is communal; and while abortion is a serious wrong, all of our sins collectively weaken and tear down the Body of Christ. Saint Paul proclaims, "All the parts of the Body of Christ should have concern for one another," and "If one part suffers, all the parts suffer with it; if one part is honored, all the parts share its joy." The rest of us need to make a commitment not to condemn, but to prayerfully ask God to send forgiveness, reconciliation, peace, and healing to all who may be suffering because of abortion.

The prophet Jeremiah wrote, "In Ramah is heard the sound of moaning, of bitter weeping! Rachel mourns her children, she refuses to be consoled because her children are no more." That's despair. But Jesus proclaims liberty to those held captive by the aftermath of abortion. That's hope.

Deacon Tom Shares Feedback He Received from His Sermon:

When I delivered this homily, at two out of four Masses I actually received applause. I was told privately by a number of different people that they cringed when they hear the topic of abortion introduced. They expressed that they had heard too many homilies condemning those who have had abortions. Many said after hearing the homily, they felt it was hopeful and healing. I had several people ask for copies because someone they knew was suffering after abortion.

As a preacher, I felt the most compelling statistic presented in the homily was that surveys at abortion sites by the Alan Guttmacher Institute of women on the day of their abortion found 34 percent in 1994 and 27 percent in 2001 admitted they were Catholics. (How many more were Catholic but too ashamed to admit it?) Also, 30 percent of Evangelical (pro-life) Protestant women are post-abortive. I felt one-third of the women who heard my homily could have been post-abortive, and this did not include the fathers/husbands present. Realizing that, I felt a homily on this subject was absolutely necessary. I had been at this church for 16 years, and had heard abortion mentioned in passing, but never the whole homily directed at the topic.

SERMON II:

[A message on healing after abortion by Kevin Burke offered after communion services.]

When I was looking for a theme for a book I was writing about men who were part of abortion decisions, and how that experience impacted them as men and fathers, the life of Peter seemed the perfect place to start...the book is called **Tears of the Fisherman.** We are blessed that Jesus chose Peter the Apostle to be his rock, the human foundation of our Church.

Those dark days of holy week were a painful and intense process of transformation for Peter that reached a climax after the resurrection of Christ at the shores of Galilee. Remember at the last supper when Jesus shares of his impending arrest and execution Peter proclaims "I will follow you to prison and die for you Master!" Just a few short hours later all hell is breaking loose – Jesus is arrested, beaten and abused by Temple guards and facing the humiliating torture of Roman scourging and Crucifixion.

Peter follows close behind as Jesus is led before the religious authorities assembled for a trial at the residence of the High Priest. When confronted in the High Priests courtyard about his association with Jesus, Peter is afraid of facing the same fate as Jesus...and he denies 3 times any association with the very one he pledged to protect – he abandoned his pledge to suffer and die with Jesus.

This healing of Peter's traumatic denial began with the bitter

tears Peter shed on that Good Friday as he faced his weakness and fear... and as he watched from afar as Jesus was crucified. That grieving experience, humbly facing that pain, was essential to his vocation in Christ.
And this healing and restoration of Peter continued with the resurrection when Jesus appeared to Peter and the 12 – and said, "Don't be afraid." Jesus knew they were frightened – and some of these men, like Peter, surely felt guilt and shame and fear of judgment.

But Peter's emotional and spiritual wounds would require an even deeper healing encounter with Jesus. Jesus appeared to Peter and the other apostles by the shores of the Sea of Galilee as they were fishing early in the morning, this place where Jesus first called him to be a fisher of men.

Jesus provided an opportunity for Peter to pledge his love for Christ and the Church three times ...healing this deep wound of his denial on that painful Good Friday.

As Pope Emeritus Benedict XVI shared:

> "The school of faith is not a triumphal march but a journey marked daily by suffering and love, trials and faithfulness. Peter, who promised absolute fidelity, knew the bitterness and humiliation of denial: the arrogant man learns the costly lesson of humility. Peter, too, must learn that he is weak and in need of forgiveness. Once his attitude changes and he understands the truth ... he weeps in ...liberating repentance... he is finally ready for his mission."[63]

Now we return to the present day. Men and women who have been part of abortion decisions in their past understand the pain of Peter...and his experience is one of great hope for us. I have a "Peter" experience in my past.

---

63 Pope Benedict XVI, General Audience, 24 May 2006

I had the beginning of a religious awakening in my college years but the abortion issue was not on the radar. I was not pro-life or pro-abortion at the time.

As I was about to begin my first year of graduate studies to become a social work counselor and a friend I was close to approached me about her unplanned pregnancy.

I told her I would respect and support her whatever she decided. If she was open to parenting or adoption, I could connect her with someone from Catholic Charities who could help.

I was unable to do what was needed at the time – to be strong in my encouragement of her maintaining the pregnancy. I failed to tell her that I understand her anxiety and fears of this unplanned pregnancy, but the pregnancy and her child were an "unexpected blessing" and the truth is… she would be a great mother.

I should have told her she is already a mother to that child in her womb, and while she would face challenges, she would not regret having this child.

I could have made an appointment with a pregnancy counselor and accompanied her to show that I was going to be an ongoing source of support to her in her decision to give life to this child.

At that time I suppose I had absorbed the professional value of the counseling profession to maintain neutral objectivity and allow her to make her own decision. I also did not want her to resent me later if she felt burdened with a child and blamed me for advocating strongly for her not to abort.

She decided to have the procedure. Years later when I learned more about how abortion hurts women and men, I came to understand how this impacted her, and I could see the clear symptoms in her life. It broke my heart.

171

I attended an RV retreat for reconciliation and healing of my role in this child's death and the wounding of the mother. I later shared with her my apologies and regret and information on Rachel's Vineyard for her to consider... I will share more about RV in a minute.

I hope that others will reflect and pray about their own role in the abortion decisions of friends and relatives, and if they have played some part in the death of the unborn.

Perhaps you are a man or woman with this loss in your past, and sometimes there's a nagging sense of guilt and shame – sometimes you think of that child that was never born. You may be a grandparent that lost grandchildren to abortion – you may struggle with your role in your son or daughter's decision – you may have been powerless to prevent the abortion and this has wounded you. RV is for you.

You may have, like me, helped a friend, a sister, cousin with their abortion; helped pay for it, drove them to the abortion center, advised them abortion was the sensible and best solution to their unplanned pregnancy...maybe you stayed silent... RV is for you as well.

Sometimes a woman or man will attend the weekend with their spouse, who may or may not be the father/mother of the child. This can be a beautiful experience of healing for their relationship. The past abortion of a spouse can impact marital life, communication, trust, and intimacy. Healing can help open the door to building a healthier relationship. Couples are welcome on RV.

The RV weekend is a beautiful and powerful experience of the mercy and forgiveness of God in a process that is specially designed to help you safely open up this part of your past, to journey with others who understand your loss. It is very much like the encounter of Peter with Jesus after the resurrection. Jesus knows we are afraid to open up this dark area of our past – he knows we need his peace but we often recoil from the light, from his invitation to healing.

The RV weekend features special scripture meditations and exercises that go to the heart of this wound, and bring the light and peace of Christ. The sacraments of reconciliation and Eucharist are part of the weekend journey.

Each retreat team has a priest and counselor as well as women and men who have experienced abortion and are there to offer support and encouragement.

You can read more about us and find retreats in your area, in this region, across the US, and around the world at RV.org.

Here's a testimony that is typical of those that attend the weekend:

A woman shares

> "This weekend I met other women and men who suffered for many years as I have, and I don't feel so alone anymore with this part of my past. The healing I experienced as the weekend unfolded was amazing…and still ongoing."

A man shares:

> "I went to the weekend not really sure how abortion had impacted my life, but open to learning more and felt like it was a time in my life to take a leap of faith. As the weekend progressed, we shared the story of our abortion (and some of us had multiple abortions)

> … And I realized just how intimately that experience hurt me as a man, emotionally, spiritually, in my relationship with those I love. I have such a deep peace now in that place of hurt, and can see many blessings unfolding in my life now a year after the retreat."

Emma Boe is a Respect Life Director in Florida and heads up the RV outreach there for many years. She shares about one of the fruits of God's mercy and healing:

"Many of our RV participants stay in touch and we can see how that healing takes root in their lives - as they grow in faith, and as a fruit of their healing, I see them getting involved in their parish or diocese in different ways; as catechists, attending or hosting bible studies and prayer groups, outreach to the poor and homeless, prison ministry, pro-life and abortion recovery ministry."

Given the numbers impacted since the procedure was legalized in 1973, there is a great harvest for the Church.

If your heart has been touched today, if the Holy Spirit is awakening hunger for this type of healing of your past, consider an RV retreat. In closing, let me share that I am so grateful for your Pastor's kindness in allowing me to speak with you today. May the love and peace of Jesus Christ be with you today and always.

SERMON III:
God is Love

[Father Peter Cipriani, of the Diocese of Bridgeport, CT., is a graduate of the North American College in Rome and is a high school teacher and chaplain at Notre Dame High School in Fairfield, CT. The following sermon was offered on a Rachel's Vineyard Retreat held in the Bridgeport Diocese.]

It is the question that will have the most significance in our lives: "Who do you say that I am?" Perhaps this is precisely the question that has brought all of you together this weekend. Searching for the truth that will not be hidden within our doubts and pains, which seem to provide us with the kinds of answers that would have us flee from God. When hemmed in by a wall of pain, fear, and anxiety, it is difficult to find within ourselves the right answers, the kinds that will lead us to peace, healing, and confidence.

Relying on ourselves in this condition is like relying on a road map of New York as you continue to get more lost in Nebraska. In such instances, one can look to Saint John who emphatically declares: "God is love." But what if my experiences of love have been anything but love…if God is love, then He is hurtful, absent and unforgiving…according to my unfortunate run-ins with so-called love.
Another Saint, who himself, had to travel perhaps one of the most difficult and demanding roads of all, having been no stranger to the needs of peace and healing, will assist us: Saint Paul.

Saint Paul was involved in countless situations where at his instigation, lives were lost, families destroyed, and people unfairly imprisoned. After being knocked off his horse and having been enveloped in the arms of the risen Christ who appeared to him on his way to Damascus, Paul would embark on a long and most worthwhile journey of healing and faith…you have this weekend of Rachel's Vineyard, Paul had about three years of a similar Rachel's Vineyard-like retreat.

And maybe it was because of the depth of his pain and sorrow that Saint Paul was able to discover the true identity of God in Christ. It is true that the deeper one descends into the darkness the more luminous and beautiful the heavens appear. Having sounded the depths of guilt and shame, sin and sorrow, Paul was able to sound the deeper, the infinite depths of God's healing mercy and unconditional love.

If he did not, how could he pen what is considered the most beautiful and perhaps most quoted passage in Scripture:

175

"Love is patient, love is kind. It is not jealous, (love) is not pompous, it is not inflated, it is not rude, it does not seek its own interests, it is not quick-tempered, it does not brood over injury, it does not rejoice over wrongdoing but rejoices with the truth. It bears all things, believes all things, hopes all things, endures all things."

One might be tempted to assign this passage as an example of how humans love. However, the bar seems to be raised so high that only someone who is perfect could possibly satisfy these incredible demands of love. And there is one, actually three, who are perfectly able to do so: The Father, Son, and Holy Spirit.

For the sake of this life and heart transforming truth, it is essential that we look at a few of these characteristics that define who God is. Love is patient. In Jeremiah we hear: "Before I formed you in the womb...I knew you." If God is love, then knowledge is the foundation of that love...God knows because He loves.

Therefore, He has loved you and promises, specifically with Jeremiah, to love you for all eternity...God does not begin to love once there is a universe in place and people to populate it, or once we make the right decision or perform a good deed. Therefore, He has always been aware of every single second of our lives, every single decision. Though we might protest: "He has known all about my sins...my most serious."

Yes, but at the same time He sees our sins, He recognizes and sees our courageous contrition...you being there on a retreat...and as Saint Paul reminds us: "He does not brood over injury or rejoice in wrongdoing as though that were the focus of His eternal gaze; rather, He rejoices in the truth... in the truth of your desire to heal, focuses on you who have come so courageously through the valley of darkness into the light of His love and kindness can now be an instrument of healing for others. The Love who is God bears all things in patience and kindness because He has had all eternity to do so. Our passing earthly lives and even the worst of our passing earthly decisions cannot impede the power and beauty of God's eternal love for you and me.

With Saint Paul, none knew the beauty and liberation of this truth greater than the Holy Virgin. Today's invitation to authentic or reclaimed discipleship on the part of Christ may make us hesitate for a moment: "Whoever wishes to come after me must deny himself, take up His cross and follow me." In the movie, *The Passion*, director Mel Gibson highlights this reality during the way of the Cross where Mary slides her way through the crowd to accompany her Son when she spots Satan as he parallels her movements on the other side of the crowd.

She recognizes her antagonist, looks at him for a moment, and then fixes her gaze on her suffering Son. Mary is participating in the sufferings of Christ as we are all called to do. Even if it is a Cross of our own manufacturing, a burden of terrible weight that we have brought upon ourselves, Christ wants you to pick up that cross, *especially that Cross* and follow after Him.

If not, what are we to say of the good thief who had fashioned his own cross through his own decisions. Jesus rejoicing in the truth of contrition replies to him: "I solemnly assure you, this day you will be with me in Paradise." A Rachel's Vineyard moment for the good thief on the Cross. This day...hear those words...not next year, next century, **but this very day.**

It is through suffering that we are saved. And unless there is the recognition of sin in our lives, then we deprive Christ of His most cherished title of Savior. It is not a title He begrudges us, as though His love for us is an obnoxious

177

bother. Imagine if someone deprived you of your title of friend. I did not want to burden you with my problems...we would feel rejected certainly, desperate to want to help one who is in trouble.

Jesus could have most certainly chosen to redeem us all by Himself, in which case He would have dispensed with Mary and the Apostles, eventually all the Saints and today with you and I. In Christ's Humanity, God extends the hand of both family unity and friendship. And what are friends and family about if not loving, living and sharing together, especially the most difficult and challenging moments of one's life?

You see, Jesus is desperate for your sufferings, He needs your sufferings, for without them He cannot redeem and save. This is the paradox of our faith... if Adam and Eve had not fallen, how could we have truly appreciated the depths of our Lord's love for us if there were no Incarnation, Passion, and Resurrection? Do we not more appreciate the spring, when the winter is ferocious and seems to go on and on with its seemingly endless darkness and cold?

Gibson once more masterfully visualizes this reality: The scourging has concluded, and Mary is inspired to soak up the blood of the Savior with linens. And seeing this example of Mary, Mary Magdalene assists her, knowing with the Holy Virgin that each drop of that precious blood when applied to one's wounds soothes and heals flesh and bone, right through to one's heart and soul.

These moments are why we gather for Mass each week. The elevation of the Host and chalice, the Body and Blood of Christ, to the Father is the moment of Calvary once more, but now we are present having brought our Cross and having it placed beside that of Jesus. Each Mass is then our offering, the offering of our lives, our loves, our joys, our sufferings, and, yes, our sins for the life of the world. We soak up the blood of Christ with the linen of our prayers and we apply its redemptive, healing power to ourselves and all those who rely on our prayers.

If God is love, then the perfect expression of that Love is Calvary. And what awaits us there is no condemnation, but salvation because Saint Paul and the Holy Virgin know who exactly God is: He is the one who bears all things, believes all things, hopes all things, endures all things.

SERMON IV:
Underestimating God's Mercy
Especially in Forgiving Abortion

[Fr. Ross Laframboise is a Priest of the Diocese of Fargo, North Dakota ordained in June 2003. He is currently assigned as parochial vicar at Little Flower Parish in Rugby, ND.

He has worked with the Diocese of Crookston and served on the Fargo Rachel's Vineyard team.]

The Father waits. Grasp for a moment the emotions rooted in the Father's heart as he waits for his prodigal son to return home from his life of debauchery. All the biblical account tells us in Luke 15:11-32 is his reaction upon the son's return. To the amazement of many, the Father embraces and kisses him.

Does the Father not know of the terrible sin this man has done! The son's coming to his father and his confession elicit not condemnation and shame but an embrace and kiss. Is such a response possible when we have sinned in grievous ways?

Jesus' description clearly illustrates that our heavenly Father is eager to pour out his mercy; we just have to return to

179

him. This image of God shatters our concept of God. In our shame of having done terribly bad things, we hide and hurt because we don't think it is possible to find healing and restoration. In grief, we fail to realize that our heavenly Father waits.

There is a strong parallel to the pain of having suffered an abortion. Years often pass, yet with two intense emotions remaining, one felt by you who, although you may have "moved on," you still feel your heartache for a child or guilt of denied motherhood or fatherhood. Yet another heart burns with equaling intensity. God the Father's heart burns with a longing to offer you love and wholeness you so much need but are unable to accept.

God the Father longs to forgive and bring to himself every woman or man who has experienced an abortion, no matter what the reason. Unfortunately, the women and men who have experienced abortion are now victims of the lie that either there was no harm done so just forget about it, or that there is no one to forgive you, no peace to find. Both lies leave you with a tragic moment buried in the past that truly needs healing and grace for you to find true happiness again.

As a new priest, I have been deeply struck by God's mercy and how it is ourselves who limit this love simply because we think God cannot or will not forgive us.

Maybe we see the unforgiveness in other human beings, maybe in our family, and we think God is the same. NOT! A far greater concern is not the sin itself but the separation and the longing in the Father's heart for you to be whole and happy again by allowing him to hug and kiss you. I do not believe God meditates on the terrible things his son or daughter has done, but rather the pain of that separation, that desire to embrace once again his beloved child.

While this applies to much of our life, I think it applies

specifically to the hurt and hidden pain so many carry around because of an abortion we have committed or allowed to happen. Buried in our society and in our hearts, are the grief and unforgiveness. You are not alone in your pain. More than four out of every ten women in the childbearing years have had an abortion. I say this not to condemn, but to make aware of the enormous amount of pain that is buried and repressed all around us. Compassion must ensue when up to 70 percent of women who have abortions do so against their own self-admitted moral principles because of a variety of fears and pressures.

What can you do with your abortion experience? Seek healing. Remember the prodigal son debated whether or not to go back because he didn't know if his father would accept him back. You know that your heavenly Father has been waiting to reach out in forgiveness and love. As humans, we know how it is to wait for someone to come back. How much more profound is the waiting for our God who loves us so intensely. The sacrament of Reconciliation is a key step. You may also desire the compassion and further help of another through the Project Rachel program or by making a Rachel's Vineyard retreat attended by others who have had an abortion and seek healing.

Along with the prodigal son, our human experience greatly underestimates the mercy and love within our heavenly Father's heart. This so often stops us from receiving the healing and love our hearts so dearly need after our worst sins. The pain and silence have gone on long enough. Please seek help for yourself or for others in which you are in contact. The Father waits.

Kevin Burke, LSW • Theresa Burke, Ph.D • Rev. Frank Pavone

SERMON V:
All Men Were Created Equal

[Deacon Chris Thompson was ordained in 2003 and serves at Our Lady of the Assumption (OLA) parish in Atlanta, Georgia. He is involved in many ministries at OLA and currently serves on the staff with his wife Cindy as the head of the parish school of religion. Since 2005 he has been blessed to participate in local Rachel's Vineyard retreats with his sister, Sister Pat Thompson, and a host of other gifted facilitators at PATH (Post Abortion Treatment and Healing). Deacon Chris can be contacted via email at: chris.thompson@gatech.edu.]

This week we remember two very important days in the history of our country. On Monday we celebrate the triumph of justice over inequality and prejudice as we remember the birth of Martin Luther King Jr., the herald of civil rights in America. Dr. King once spoke of a dream when all peoples would stand together.

In perhaps his most famous speech he proclaimed:

I have a dream that one day this nation will rise up and live out the true meaning of its creed:
"We hold these truths to be self-evident that all men are created equal and this will be the day -- this will be the day when all of God's children will be able to sing with new meaning: My country 'tis of thee, sweet land of liberty, of thee I sing."

Unfortunately, that time has not yet arrived for everyone.

On January 22, we also remember the anniversary of Roe vs. Wade and the legalization of abortion in America. Since then millions of children have perished, and countless mothers, fathers, grandparents, and families have suffered great guilt, pain, and distress over the loss of their children and grandchildren due to their "choice."

The chances are great that many of those touched by abortion in some way are sitting right here in our church on any given Sunday.

In the Gospel today, John the Baptist said of Jesus,

"Behold, the Lamb of God, Who takes away the sin of the world."

More than anything else I want anyone touched by abortion to know and BELIEVE that Jesus loves you and has already forgiven you. He is waiting with open arms for you to accept this love and forgiveness. And your children or grandchildren, who live forever in the loving presence of God, have forgiven you as well.

In the Gospel of Life John Paul II wrote:

"The Church is aware of the many factors which may have influenced your decision, and she does not doubt that in many cases it was a painful and even shattering decision. The wound in your heart may not yet have healed. Certainly what happened was and remains terribly wrong. But do not give in to discouragement and do not lose hope.

Try rather understanding what happened and face it honestly. If you have not already done so, give yourselves over with humility and trust to repentance. The Father of mercies is ready to give you his forgiveness and his peace in the Sacrament of Reconciliation. To the same Father and to his mercy you can with sure hope entrust your child. With the friendly and expert help and advice of other people, and as a result of your own painful experience, you can be among the most eloquent defenders of everyone's right to life. Through your commitment to life, whether by accepting the birth of other children or by welcoming and caring for those

183

most in need of someone to be close to them, you will become promoters of a new way of looking at human life."

I have experienced firsthand the pain of women and men, husbands and wives, families and relatives who have suffered from abortion. I have seen the courage, struggle, and eventual healing of those who seek to reconcile themselves with God about this issue. Through a weekend-long retreat called Rachel's Vineyard, the true mercy and presence of God are experienced through Scripture and prayer.

I will never forget the experience of watching Christ work multiple miracles of healing unfold right in front of my eyes. If you know of anyone suffering from the aftereffects of abortion, either directly or indirectly, please encourage them to contact the post-abortion-healing insert in today's bulletin.

In the Gospel of Life John Paul II went on to write:

"There can be no *true democracy* without a recognition of every person's dignity and without respect for his or her rights. Nor can there be true peace unless *life is defended and promoted.*"

If Dr. King were alive at the time I feel sure he would have stood beside John Paul and asked us to remember that every aborted life, without a name and without a grave, was meant by God to make a difference...so too are we called to make a difference.

Many who defend abortion believe they are protecting the right to make a choice. Many contemplating abortion believe they have no othe4 choice.

Many recovering fr0-*om abortion believe they have no chance of being whole again.

We must listen to them all.

We must try to understand their sense of isolation and despair.

We must strive to know their hearts.

We must offer them hope and forgiveness.

We must pray without ceasing for an end to the tragedy that began [in 1973].

As we come forward to receive the Eucharist today, let us pray that WE might become instruments of God's mercy and forgiveness.

As Father Lopez wrote:

Lord Jesus, you came to show us the way home to the Father.

We ask you to pour the power of Your grace into the minds and hearts of those who would show the path to healing for all those who suffer because of abortion.

Set our hearts on fire with the love of your Sacred Heart so that no one we meet,

crushed by pain, guilt, or grief will be beyond your saving touch. Awaken our minds to understand, touch our lips with your wisdom, and fill our hearts with such courage that no attitude, no person, no situation will keep us from being your means of mercy.

Amen.

Kevin Burke, LSW • Theresa Burke, Ph.D • Rev. Frank Pavone

RESOURCES FOR RECOVERY

Rachel's Vineyard
An International Ministry of Priests for Life

**Weekend Retreats and Support Groups
for Healing After Abortion**
www.RachelsVineyard.org
1-877-HOPE-4-ME

Rachel's Vineyard

National Office:
808 N. Henderson Rd.
King of Prussia, PA 19406
(ph) 610-354-0555 (fax) 610-354-0311

An Invitation to Healing…

Rachel's Vineyard is a safe place to heal hearts broken
by abortion. Weekend retreats offer you a supportive,
confidential, and non-judgmental environment where
women and men can reconcile painful emotions and
begin the process of healing after abortion.

Rachel's Vineyard creates a place where men and
women can share, often for the first time, their deepest
feelings about abortion. You are allowed to dismantle
troubling secrets in an environment of emotional and

spiritual safety.

Rachel's Vineyard is a therapy for the soul. Participants, who have been trapped in anger towards themselves or others, experience forgiveness. Peace is found. Lives are restored. A sense of hope and meaning for the future is finally re-discovered.

If you or someone you know is in need of healing after abortion, we invite you to look at our website **www. RachelsVineyard.org**, *to find a retreat site near you and continue your healing journey. You are also welcome to call our hotline,* **1-877-HOPE-4-ME** *to get in touch with your local Rachel's Vineyard site leader.*

Rachel's Vineyard Ministries
Pregnancy Loss and Unresolved Grief

Clinical Training Seminars

Join the pioneers and experts in the abortion recovery movement for a dynamic and life-changing day of training that will build and strengthen a solid foundation for Healing After Abortion!

· Approved Education Credits for:
  Clergy
  Psychologists
  Counselors
  Therapists
  Social Workers
  Nurses
  Pastoral Care Ministers
  Students

General Public

Rachel's Vineyard, an International Ministry of Priests
For Life, has revolutionized the field of counseling after
abortion, providing an outstanding empirically validated treatment model for Evangelization and healing.

To arrange a training opportunity near you, contact:

Theresa Burke, Ph.D.
Phone: 610-354-0555
Email: travel@rachelsvineyard.org

Silent No More Awareness Campaign

Christians make the public aware of the
devastation abortion brings to wom-
en and men. The campaign seeks to
expose and heal the secrecy and silence
surrounding the emotional and physical pain of abortion. The Campaign is a
project of Priests for Life and Anglicans for Life.

www.AbortionForgiveness.com
*(Zipcode generated site to find abortion healing pro-
grams in your area.)*
Web: www.SilentNoMore.com
Email: mail@silentnomore.com
Phone: 412-749-0455

SaveOne

SAVEONE

Helping men, women, and families recover after an
abortion. SaveOne offers help for men, women, and

family members/friends, through group study, online study, or answering questions and giving encouragement through self-study and a Bible-based curriculum that was written by founder Sheila Harper.
SaveOne.org
615 347 8800

Forgiven and Set Free

Publisher: Baker Books; Revised,
Updated edition (May 19, 2015)
Abortion healing Bible Study by Linda Cochrane

Men and Abortion Network

www.lifeissues.org/men
The Men and Abortion
Network (MAN) has a website exclusively for men who grieve after the loss of a child to abortion. Access to a free peer-to-peer counselor is available near them and the website hosts a wide selection of resources, some of them free, that will help men find a path to recovery, hope, and peace.

Project Joseph

Project Joseph is a life-changing opportunity for men who struggle with the emotional and spiritual pain of abortion. This one-day retreat is a unique and effective process designed specifically to help men experience the mercy and compassion of God.
www.projectjoseph.org

Project Rachel

www.hopeafterabortion.com

BOOKS

Forbidden Grief
The Unspoken Pain of Abortion

By Theresa Burke with
David Reardon (Acorn Books).

Recognizing abortion as trauma in
a person's life, this compelling work
uniquely examines the psychological
impact of induced abortion. It reflects
in-depth insight and clinical exam-
ples of how abortion may affect one's
self-concept. It includes dozens of
vignettes with psychological inter-
pretation, excerpts from women's diaries and letters. It
will validate the feelings of loss and shame experienced
by many - presenting a name for their pain and helping them make sense of the 'self-destructive' behaviors
which often follow abortion.

For the clinician, Forbidden Grief provides a detailed
explanation of how feelings, emotions and even psycho-
physiological symptoms are related to abortion trauma
through eating disorders, anxiety and panic responses,
depression, and conflicts with maternal identity. Further, abortion itself may re-enact the trauma of former
sexual abuse. These are important concepts to be aware
of when dealing with post-aborted women and men. It
can help them to understand self-destructive tendencies that often unconsciously follow trauma. This book

will give you a detailed understanding of post-abortion symptoms and the many levels of traumatic impact.

Order information:
Tel. 321-500-1000
www.prolifeproducts.org

Tears of the Fisherman
Recovery for Men Wounded by Abortion

By Kevin Burke, LSW

Order Information:
www.tearsofthefisherman.com
Tel. 321-500-1000
www.prolifeproducts.org

Shockwaves
Abortion's Wider Circle of Victims

Janet Morana, co-founder of Silent No More, shines a bright light on the undeniable truth of abortion, that it impacts everyone. Besides killing the baby, it affects moms, dads, grandparents, siblings, the whole family, friends, abortionists, and pro-life activists. With 60 million legal abortions since 1973, there's no segment of our nation untouched.

Order Information:
Tel. 321-500-1000
www.prolifeproducts.org

The Contraception of Grief
The Genesis of Anguish Conceived by Abortifacients
and Sterilization

By Theresa Burke, Ph.D.
With contributions by Janet Morana,
PD, Steve Harmon, Susan Gliko and
Kevin Burke, LSW

This book exposes the pain that so
many women endure when they realize that the contraceptives they used
caused the deaths of their children.
This book is for women, men, pastors,
doctors and all who minister to the family.

Order Information:
Tel. 321-500-1000
www.prolifeproducts.org

A Gift of Time

By Amy Kuebelbeck & Deborah L.
Davis, Ph.D

A Gift of Time is a gentle and practical guide for parents who decide to
continue their pregnancy knowing
that their baby's life will be brief.
When prenatal testing reveals that
an unborn child is expected to die
before or shortly after birth, some
parents will choose to proceed with the pregnancy and
to welcome their child into the world. With compassion
and support, A Gift of Time walks them step-by-step

through this challenging and emotional experience – from the infant's life-limiting prenatal diagnosis and the decision to have the baby to coping with the pregnancy and making plans for the baby's birth and death.

Finding You

From Sheila Harper at SaveOne (www.saveone.org) "Finding You" is a guide as well as a Bible study for men and women seeking healing and freedom from the after-effects of sexual trauma. Whether the abuse happened 10, 20, or 50 years ago, you can put away this trauma and reframe your thoughts concerning this time in your life.

Heart Cries and Healing

By Karen Stevenson, MD, M Div

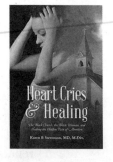

Heart Cries and Healing: The Black Church, The Black Woman, and Healing the Hidden Pain of Abortion tells the untold story about abortion and the African American community. It explores the historical, cultural, and community influences that have resulted in the epidemic numbers of abortion in the black community. It is the story that the community has refused to acknowledge and tell; and because of this refusal, there remains an unhealed wound that is both hidden and yet expressed in a multitude of ways.

Rivers of Blood / Oceans of Mercy

Kevin Burke, LSW • Theresa Burke, Ph.D • Rev. Frank Pavone

ABOUT THE AUTHORS

THERESA BURKE, Ph.D., is the founder of The Rachel's Vineyard™ support group and retreat models now offered in 49 states and over 70 countries. Theresa is a Pastoral Associate of Priests for Life and has lectured and trained professionals internationally on the subject of post-abortion trauma and healing. Dr. Burke's healing programs offer a unique sensory based treatment which integrates emotional, psychological and spiritual dimensions for those suffering after abortion, sexual abuse, and other trauma. Her books include *Forbidden Grief - The Unspoken Pain of Abortion* with David C. Reardon (Acorn Books), and *The Contraception of Grief* – The Genesis of Anguish Conceived by Abortifacients and Sterilization.

KEVIN BURKE is a licensed social worker, Co-Founder of Rachel's Vineyard Ministries and a Pastoral Associate of Priests for Life. Kevin's presentations address the effects of abortion on men, couples and families and effective post abortion ministry for Clergy and Counselors. Kevin is the author of *Tears of the Fisherman: Recovery for Men Wounded by Abortion.* He has contributed to and authored articles on the trauma and recovery after abortion, and as a musician and songwriter, uses the gift of music as an effective way to educate the public, and share a message of hope and healing. Kevin has been a guest on EWTN's "At Home with Jim and Joy" and the "Gospel of Life" on Sky Angel Network. He is a regular guest on national radio shows.

FR. FRANK PAVONE is one of the most prominent pro-life leaders in the world. He became a Catholic priest in 1988 under Cardinal John O'Connor in New York. In 1993 he became National Director of Priests for Life. He is also the President of the National Pro-life Religious Council, and the National Pastoral Director of the Silent No More Awareness Campaign and of Rachel's Vineyard. He travels to several states each week, preaching and teaching against abortion. He broadcasts regularly on television, radio and internet. He was asked by Mother Teresa to speak in India on abortion, and has served at the Vatican as an official of the Pontifical Council for the Family, helping coordinate the pro-life activities of the Catholic Church.

ABOUT OUR MINISTRY

Priests for Life, the ministry under whose auspices this book is published and on the pastoral team of which its three authors serve, is the largest ministry, shaped by Catholic principles, that is focused exclusively on ending abortion and healing its wounds.

The Priests for Life family of ministries, which you can see at www.ProLifeCentral.com, provides a strong focus on healing after abortion, and includes Rachel's Vineyard and the Silent No More Awareness Campaign.

The Prayer Campaign of Priests for Life includes many prayers for healing (see www.ProLifePrayers.com), summarized in such booklets as *In the Heart of His Mercy*, available on our online store at ProLifeProducts.org.

Whether you are a member of the clergy or the laity, and whether you are Catholic or of another religious persuasion, you are welcome to join the efforts of Priests for Life and its related ministries. For more information, contact

Priests for Life
PO Box 236695 • Cocoa, FL 32923
Tel. 321-500-1000, Email: mail@priestsforlife.org
www.ProLifeCentral.com
Support us at: ProLifeDonation.com